OUT OF THE MISTS OF TIME:

Who Wrote the Bible and Why

With Best Wishes

Milton L. Forbes

OUT OF THE MISTS OF TIME:

Who Wrote the Bible and Why

by

Milton L. Forbes

Mountaintop Books
GLENWOOD, IOWA

Thanks to Marcia B. Forbes for many valuable suggestions.

Book manufactured by
Thomson-Shore
7300 West Joy Road
Dexter, Michigan 48130

Published by
Mountaintop Books
P.O. Box 385
Glenwood, Iowa 51534-0385.

Library of Congress Catalog Card Number 91-91561
ISBN 0-9623700-2-9

CONTENTS

And Hilkiah the high priest said unto
Shaphan the scribe,
I have found the book of the law
in the house of the Lord...

And Shaphan read it before the king...
And... the king... rent his clothes...

Thus said the Lord,
Behold, I will bring evil upon this place...

And the king stood by a pillar,
and made a covenant before the Lord...
to perform the words of the covenant
that were written in this book...

And like unto him was there no king before him,
that turned to the Lord with all his heart,
and with all his soul, and with all his might,
according to all the law of Moses;
neither after him arose there any like him.

—2 Kings 22:8-23:25

1

A Search for Meaning

If the Bible is important, it is important to read it intelligently. *Out of the Mists of Time: Who Wrote the Bible and Why* is about understanding what the many writers were trying to say, in the books that became the Bible. Like all of us, each author was a prisoner of a definite time, place, and culture even while reaching for the stars.

Countless passages in the Bible seem mysterious. But with a little careful reading and some help from knowledgeable sources, we can often discover the author's intended meaning.

Ezekiel

For example, the following verses from the book of Ezekiel provide considerable information that is not immediately obvious.

"Now it came to pass in the thirtieth year, in the fourth month, in the fifth day of the month, as I was among the captives by the river of Chebar, that the heavens were opened, and I saw visions of God" (Ezek. 1:1).

It is clear that Ezekiel saw visions of God, and that he saw them in the thirtieth year. The thirtieth year of what? Scholars of Hebrew are not certain, but most agree that it *probably* means that he was thirty years old. Some uncertainties will forever remain.

Who were the captives? We find out from the next two verses:

"In the fifth day of the month, which was the fifth year of King Jehoiachin's captivity, the word of the Lord came expressly unto Ezekiel the priest, the son of Buzi, in the land of the Chaldeans by the river Chebar; and the hand of the Lord was there upon him" (Ezek. 1:2-3).

The land of the Chaldeans was Babylonia. The Babylonians took Jehoiachin, king of Judah and Israel, to their own country, along with ten thousand other captives (2 Kings 24:10-16). The year of exile was 597 BC, according to historians; therefore, Ezekiel's visions began in 592 BC.

What was the river of Chebar? Not a river, the Chebar still exists as the *nahr el-qebir*, a large canal near the ruins of Nippur in southern Iraq.

Notice that Ezekiel did not write verses two and three; an editor composed them and inserted them into the text to introduce Ezekiel to future students. After the editor's introduction, Ezekiel tells about the visions that he saw in the fifth year of King Jehoiachin's captivity (Ezek. 1:4 on). The revelations of the fifth year continue through several chapters, until he introduces his visions of the sixth year (Ezek. 8:1). And so on for the whole book. Evidently other people did not see the visions, but many came to hear him speak (Ezek. 8:1, 14:1, 20:1).

Chapters 26 to 30 are out of order: chapter 26 tells of visions that Ezekiel saw the eleventh year, but chapter 29 goes back to the tenth year. Why are they out of sequence? One explanation is that at some time the scroll came apart, or vandals tore it up, then a caretaker lovingly reassembled the pieces the best way that he could. Sometimes the fragments were not put back in the original order.

Repeated editing over hundreds of years could have produced a similar effect. Many sections appear to have been composed on specific topics and inserted into the text. An example is the note about Ezekiel's wife's death (Ezek. 24:15-

18). The verses following may have been a further addition, for they describe Ezekiel's reaction to her death (Ezek. 24:19-27).

Another possible insertion is a song in praise of Tyre's commerce (Ezek. 27:10-24). Students believe that it was composed in Tyre and placed with other material about Tyre.

There are many such evidences of editing that we cannot go into here. One of Ezekiel's disciples collected his works and wrote an introduction after he died. Long afterward, as conditions changed, others continued to write additions to represent his teachings. In that age, such pseudepigraphy was the pious work of respectable men in honor of great teachers. Today we would like to distinguish Ezekiel's actual words and to date the additions.

Survival of Ancient Scriptures

It is not surprising that such changes could happen to a book through twenty-five centuries, is it? It is amazing that it survived at all through wars, bookburnings, housecleanings, and decay. Books survived because people treasured them and handed them down generation by generation. They laboriously copied torn and crumbling pages with pen and ink, to replace them before they were lost forever. Popular books were copied more, with better chances that at least one would survive. Some were hunted down and burnt. A few books like the Dead Sea scrolls and the gnostic gospels have survived in secret hiding places.

Upon how many men has the preservation of the book of Ezekiel depended through the centuries? How many hands have laboriously copied this scroll when the papyrus was falling apart, just in time before it turned to dust? How many times has only a single copy been saved from disaster? How many times have fragments of it been pieced together to try to give the best reading? How many copyists' errors have crept in, never to be properly corrected? The Bible contains thousands of breaks due to piecing, miscopying, and editing, and they have altered and obscured the original meaning. Many sections are not clear because they were written in places and times unfamiliar to us.

Search for Meaning

Who wrote the Bible? Many different men wrote the different books of the Bible, and sections within those books. Who were they? We seldom know. Sometimes a book shows clear signs of composition centuries after the supposed author is known to have lived. The Bible was written over a time span of a thousand years, through many different periods of history. Some sections of the Old Testament contain echoes of the bronze age. The New Testament was written in the hey-day of the Roman empire. If we know when and where a particular passage was written, we can better understand what the author meant and why he said it.

The Bible is a most precious collection of books. Many readers find comfort, hope, and inspiration in them. Some look for the meaning of life; others, a guide to proper living. Still others find prophecies of things to come. Most are searching for meaning—what the author is trying to say. Some passages are thanksgivings to the Eternal; others were written in times of peril. Poets find beauty in composition, rhyme, or rhythm, especially in the original languages. Tides and storms of history have left their marks throughout the Bible, and its authors' fingerprints are on every page. And so our quest for clues to solving the mysteries of the Bible becomes a study of its authors, and of the times in which they lived.

The Different Bibles

The King James and the Catholic Bibles are versions of approximately the same collections of books. Scholars continually go back to ancient manuscripts with better methods and greater background knowledge, and so they continually produce more accurate readings. People tend to prefer the version they were brought up with, for a particular style and wording can produce an emotional hold on a person.

And there are different "Bibles." The Jewish "Bible"—the Torah, Prophets and Writings—is essentially the Old Testament of the Christian Bible. The Koran, the "Bible" of Islam, presents new revelations that build on the Torah and the teachings of Jesus. The sacred books contain poems, historical facts, tales, worldly proverbs, prescriptions for attaining eternal life. There are lamentations as well as joyful wedding songs. These books are all most precious collections of literature into which human beings have poured their hearts and souls and thoughts while reaching for infinity.

The Periods of Bible Composition

The writing of the Bible may be divided into four ages as follows.

The monarchy and the two kingdom period. The oldest sections of the Old Testament were probably written during Solomon's reign, or David's; some may have originated in the previous Canaanite empire. At any rate, writing flourished after Solomon's monarchy separated into the kingdoms of Judah and Israel in 933 BC. The two kingdom period ended when the Assyrian empire destroyed Israel in 722 BC, took the people into exile, and assimilated them.

The Deuteronomist and Deuteronomist historian. Josiah's reign, 622—609 BC, was a period of intense composition of legal and historical books in the Old Testament. The Deuteronomist and the Deuteronomist historian left their opinions all over the place, and so we will begin our examination here.

The exile and return. The Babylonian empire destroyed Judah in 597 BC and took the Israelites into exile. The exile in Babylonia was *the* exile, the great watershed in Jewish history. And they were not assimilated but *returned* from exile. Then the Jews worked at creating the holy nation of Israel-Judah, the New Israel, a model of obedience to God, to lead the whole world into an era of peace. As a guide, the priests created the Torah from the most sacred of their ancient scriptures, and wrote or finalized many other books in this period.

The age of revelation. But the cycle of empire-building, rebellion, and suppression escalated, and peace remained only a dream. Apparently, only God could end war and misery. Numerous writers found reasons to believe that God would intervene in worldly affairs only by destroying the world. That belief led them to write a mass of apocalypse, that is, a literature of the secrets which God was only now revealing as the world approached its end. The age of revelation virtually ended for the Jews when the Romans destroyed Jerusalem in 70 CE. But Paul's apocalypse of salvation spread to peoples to whom the destruction of Jerusalem meant nothing. And his age of revelation lives on.

In the chapters to follow, we will look at those four great periods of writing, but not entirely in historical sequence. We will begin with the "the book of the law" in the reign of King Josiah because its discovery provides a rare glimpse of the books that the Israelites possessed at that time.

2

"I Have Found the Book of the Law"

When Josiah, king of Judah, was twenty-six years old, he ordered the repair of Solomon's temple. It had fallen into ruin, for the heavy tribute that Assyria had demanded for the last hundred years left nothing for maintenance. Now Assyria had lost her power over Judah. In the reconstruction of the temple, the workmen found treasure and scrolls hidden in the walls.

Hilkiah the high priest examined the scrolls. One astonished him. "It is the book of the law of Moses!" he told Shaphan, the king's scribe, in surprise. "Read it!"

Shaphan read the scroll, and he also was amazed. The two discussed its significance, then Shaphan took it to the king. The king had Shaphan read it to him. As he listened, his curiosity gave way to terror, and he ripped his clothes. He sent for Hilkiah, Ahikam (Shaphan's son), Achbor (Michaiah's son), and his own servant, Asahiah. Josiah told them, "Hilkiah discovered our covenant with Yahweh. My ancestors broke the covenant! Yahweh must be furious! He must be ready to destroy us!"

Yahweh was the god of Israel. Sometimes rendered as Jehovah in English translations, his name is usually substituted by the title, "Lord."

The men agreed that the situation was dire. They consulted a woman of Yahweh, and her oracle frightened them all the more: Yahweh would destroy the nation for its disobedience. Looking for a way out, the king and his advisors conferred with the elders, who proposed that the nation renew its covenant with Yahweh in a public ceremony, and obey his commandments to the letter from that time on. Then perhaps Yahweh would not destroy the nation.

The Israelites Renew Their Covenant

So Josiah called a great assembly of all the people before the temple and read to them the book of the covenant which Hilkiah the high priest had found.

Then, standing beside a pillar, Josiah made a covenant to Yahweh on behalf of the Israelites, to carry out their side of the covenant. And all the people stood to show their commitment to their covenant with Yahweh, with all their hearts and all their souls.

Covenants with rulers. In that age, nations and nomadic tribes made treaties with their gods exactly as small nations made treaties with the kings of empires. Any such treaty with an emperor obligated the people to obey him and send him tribute. Likewise, the treaty with a god bound the people to obey every command, and required them to nourish the god with offerings of food and the smell of burnt sacrifices. Any covenant worked both ways: the emperor promised not to send in his armies to slaughter and plunder; he would shelter his vassals from other neighbors.

Similarly, a treaty with a god obliged him to protect his people from other nations, their gods, and "natural" disasters. The people would seal the covenant by reciting a list of curses against themselves to show that they understood that their master would punish them with destruction and massacre or exile, if they failed to keep their promises. Not that the people necessarily expected to see their ruling god appear in person to deliver on his promises or threats: usually he brought gentle rains, health, and peace, or disease, earth-quakes, and wars.

Josiah's Reforms. After the ceremony to renew Israel's covenant with Yahweh, Josiah commanded Hilkiah, the lower priests, and the doorkeepers to remove from the temple all the idols, altars, and trappings for the worship of Baal, Ashtoreth, sun and moon gods, planetary gods, and astral gods, and burn them in the valley of the brook Kidron outside Jerusalem. Josiah destroyed the houses of the fertility cults next to the temple. He destroyed the shrines to Ashtoreth, Chemosh, and Milcom which Solomon had built just outside Jerusalem. He destroyed Topheth, the altar to Molech. (Molech, king, was the invisible god-king who ruled the people. He was probably Yahweh.) Many men, including Josiah's grandfather, had sacrificed their own children at this altar in the valley south of the city in hope of divine protection. Josiah destroyed shrines to Yahweh and other gods throughout Judah and turned out their priests. Only Solomon's temple remained as a place of worship, and it would be devoted to Yahweh alone. He then destroyed the shrines at Beth-El and throughout Samaria. And Josiah commanded that wizards and persons who were thought to possess servant spirits be "put away." Then they held a great passover feast, "the first such" since the time of the judges, and the only one of Josiah's reign.

Thus Josiah carried out the Israelites' side of the covenant with Yahweh, in the hope that Yahweh would forgive Judah for past sins. The narrator assures us that it was done in accordance with the law of Moses. This history is taken from 2 Kings 22-23, which was also the source for the version in 2 Chron. 34-35.)

What Was the Book of the Law of Moses?

Why did Hilkiah's book of the law of Moses scare Josiah and his advisors so much that they made a new covenant and turned society upside down throughout Judah and Samaria? How could this law have been so different from the laws they already had? Hadn't Moses given them laws from God hundreds of years earlier?

Let us begin with the word "law." It is the usual Biblical translation of the Hebrew *torah*. Its use here suggests *the* Torah, which consists of the books of Genesis, Exodus, Leviticus, Numbers, and Deuteronomy. The Torah is also called the Five Books of Moses, the Pentateuch, the law of Moses, or simply the Law. Did Hilkiah discover the Torah? The Chronicler thought so, for he said that Shaphan read *extracts* from it to the king (2 Chron. 34:18).

But Shaphan read *the whole book* to the king; Josiah read *the whole book* to the assembly (2 Kings 22:10; 23:2), not five books. So it was not the Five Books of Moses, the Torah that we know. Also, the *torah* that Hilkiah found was called the book of the covenant (2 Kings 23:2), which the Torah is not. We are visiting an era before those five books existed, when *torah* meant any laws, teachings, or instruction. As we shall see in later chapters, the priests and sages probably had two other *torahs* in the tradition of Moses long before Josiah's time.

What was the *torah* that Hilkiah found? Josiah's reforms provide clues. The Israelites were to worship Yahweh alone, and him only at Solomon's temple in Jerusalem. All other sanctuaries and all idols were to be destroyed. Fertility rites were forbidden. Children were not to be sacrificed. Wizards and persons with servant spirits were to be put away. The passover was to be celebrated in commemoration of the flight from

Egypt under Moses' leadership. Where in the Bible can we find those specific regulations?

The Deuteronomic Code, or D

The part of the Bible that corresponds best with Josiah's reform is in the book of Deuteronomy (Deut. 12:1-26:15). That section is the latter part of Moses' second farewell speech before the Israelites entered Canaan. In it, Moses details Yahweh's covenant. He repeatedly demands worship of Yahweh alone, at a place which Yahweh would choose and name after himself (Deut. 12:5, 11-14, 18; 16:6, 11, 16; 26:2). That place could only be Solomon's temple in Jerusalem in Josiah's day. Moses prohibits cult prostitution (Deut. 23:17-18) and child sacrifice (Deut. 12:31, 18:10). He commands putting away wizards and anyone possessing a familiar spirit. He commands three great annual celebrations in Jerusalem. These are the passover, combined with the feast of unleavened bread, fourteen days after the new moon in March—April; the feast of firstfruits, weeks, or pentecost fifty days later; and Sukkot, the harvest feast combined with a desert ceremony of tabernacles or booths in September—October.

The king and his advisors did not know those laws, or if they did, they missed them among hundreds of laws. But after Hilkiah's discovery, they accepted the new document as the genuine law of Moses (2 Kings 23:25). Anything else previously called the law of Moses, was either incomplete or wrong. For example, child sacrifice must have been permitted or even *required* before Josiah's reform, as we shall see in chapter six.

This document, Deut. 12:1-26:15, is called the Deuteronomic code, or simply D. Many scholars believe that most of the Torah and parts of the historical books were assembled from older documents. That is the documentary hypothesis. D is one of those documents, and we will meet others.

Origin of D. The unknown person who created D is called
the Deuteronomist. Within D, repetitions and shifts from
subject to subject show that D itself had been pieced from
more ancient documents. One section must have been written
before the time of Saul and David, for it does not mention
kings though it is a war code (Deut. 20-21). From these clues
and many others, scholars have concluded that D or its
sources had been written by priests of Ephraim in the northern kingdom of Israel. The priests of Israel claimed descent
from Moses while those of Judah claimed descent from Aaron.
They had somewhat different traditions and scriptures, and
were jealously proud of their differences.

The Mosaic priests once had a temple for the worship of
Yahweh at Shiloh in Israel (1 Samuel 1:1ff) . They had an
ark, or chest, containing tablets inscribed with the ten commandments. The Philistines destroyed Shiloh and captured
the ark. The priests escaped to Nob (1 Sam. 21:1-30:7-8).

David, a shepherd from Bethlehem in Judah, helped Saul
carve out the kingdom of Israel among the northern tribes.
David was cunning and treacherous, for after a quarrel, David
fled and collaborated with the Philistine effort to pacify "wild
tribes" in Judah. The Philistines placed David over the walled
Canaanite city of Ziklag. Large landowners of Judah made him
their king about 1013 BC. Saul and his successors were killed,
and David formed a league with Israel in 1006. He shortly
took the Canaanite city-state of Jerusalem for the capital of
his united kingdom of Israel-Judah. He brought Abiathar from
Nob to Jerusalem to share priestly duties with Zadok of Judah.
After Solomon inherited the united kingdom in 973, he
banished Abiathar to Anathoth in Israel. Solomon built a
magnificent temple, and one of Yahweh's sanctuaries was
brought into it—tent and all!—over protests from Levites
nostalgic for their desert traditions (2 Sam. 7:2-7). After
Solomon died in 933, Israel and Judah separated, and their

priests had little to do with each other. The D document may have been written in Israel late in the two kingdom era.

In 726-722 BC, Assyria invaded Israel, and refugees flooded into Jerusalem. Mosaic priests among them may have brought the D document to Jerusalem at that time.

Completion of the book of Deuteronomy. D was expanded into the present book of Deuteronomy soon after Hilkiah discovered it. Moses' first farewell address was added (Deut. 1-4). The first part of his second discourse was added, including the ten commandments (Deut. 5:1-11:32), and a closing which sealed the covenant with Yahweh (Deut. 26:16-28:68). Moses' third discourse was added (Deut. 29-30), then supplemented with the ancient song of Moses (Deut. 31-32). The story of Moses' death and burial was transferred from the end of a scroll of Moses stories to the end of Deuteronomy (Deut. 34:1-6). Now Deuteronomy formed the climax and ending for the Moses stories.

Who made the additions to the D document? The clues are in the book of Jeremiah. That book is sympathetic to Josiah's reform and itemizes some of the measures. Jeremiah was Josiah's advisor and began his work in the thirteenth year of the reign. He was probably about Josiah's age. He was son of Hilkiah of the priests of Anathoth, perhaps the same Hilkiah who discovered D. Jeremiah was probably the writer-editor who added to D, forming the book of Deuteronomy.

The Greek name, "Deuteronomy," means "second law." That is a misnomer taken from the Septuagint (the Greek version of the scriptures). There "a copy of this law" was mistranslated as "a second law" (Deut. 17:18). The Hebrew name is "Words" from the first sentence, "These are the words which Moses spoke."

The Deuteronomist Historian, Dtr¹

Whoever put together the sequel to Deuteronomy (Joshua, Judges, Samuel, and Kings) had a style and viewpoint similar to the Deuteronomist's. Those books are about obedience to Yahweh as taught in Deuteronomy. The editor-writer is called the Deuteronomist historian or Dtr¹. He made additions after Josiah died and during the early part of the exile; those additions are called Dtr². Dtr¹~Dtr² was probably Jeremiah, judging by his opinions. If so, Jeremiah was a busy man. His fervent hope was that the kingdom of Judah would remain inviolate and free. That required the Israelites to do Yahweh's will so that he would protect them. Dtr¹ included stories about Yahweh's choice of David to rule the united kingdom and promised that his descendents would rule Judah forever. Dtr¹ included a prophecy that one of David's descendents who obeyed Yahweh would reunite Israel and Judah (1 Kings 11:29-39, etc.). Josiah did just that, and his reign formed the grand climax of the sequel, Joshua through Kings. We examine those books:

Joshua. Dtr¹ wrote the introduction (Joshua 1). Joshua was a popular hero remembered in many legends, and Dtr¹ represented him as a younger Moses. Dtr¹ likened Joshua's parting and crossing the Jordan to Moses' parting and crossing the Red Sea, to remind the Israelites that their life in Canaan depended on their obedience to Yahweh and his good will. Through his Joshua stories, Dtr¹ tied the ark of the covenant, circumcision, and the passover with the exodus and conquest of Canaan.

Dtr¹ collected ancient stories from Gilgal near Jericho (Joshua 2-9). There were tales about Joshua the hero leading the Israelite tribes who settled in Canaan. The stories explained such things as how the walled cities of Jericho and Ai were destroyed. Others told why twelve stones stood in the

Jordan River (the mythical twelve tribes of Israel crossed there). Those landscape features predated the conquest, but the storytellers' memories did not go back that far. The ring of twelve stones at Gilgal probably had been a Canaanite shrine. Joshua 10-12 gives a mythical account of the subduing of the Canaanites. The usually peaceful infiltration over the centuries from many directions into the collapsed Canaanite empire was misnamed the "conquest" because Dtr[1] exploited legends of the occasional battles to emphasize Yahweh's intolerance of other cults.

The Abraham, Isaac, and Jacob stories indicate that some of the Israelite tribes had come from Syria at various times. Other tribes came from the desert; several entered the Transjordan about 1250 BC. Joshua led the tribe of Joseph (Manasseh) across the Jordan into the northern central hills of Canaan about 1225 BC. Ephraim settled south of Joseph about the same time. Judah, Simeon, Caleb, and the Kenites came in from the south and settled below Jerusalem. Afterward, Benjamin settled between Jerusalem and Ephraim in conflict with its settled neighbors. Reuben, Gad, and part of Manasseh remained in the Transjordan. The Levites probably entered last and made a profession of their Yahwist cult, for they "had no land" for grazing or farming (Josh. 21). They settled in cities and villages, offering the help of their god in return for food and valuables. Their tabernacles for Yahweh were tents, and they placed them at Canaanite "high places" such as Gilgal, Shiloh, Ramah, Shechem, Gilbeah, Beth-El, and Dan.

During the period of the conquest, sheep and goat herding tribes would move into thinly inhabited hill country and cut the forests to graze and farm the land. Canaanites, physically similar and speaking a related dialect, lived in or around walled cities and farmed the surrounding plains. Sometimes they left the plains and settled in the hills like the Israelites, for throughout the hill country archaeologists have found unfortified villages on top of long-abandoned ruins or unoccupied land. Paved streets indicate that some residents had previously lived in cities of the coastal plain. Sometimes Israelites enslaved Canaanites (Josh. 9), while Canaanites in the farming country in the plain of Jezreel enslaved the tribe of Issachar (Gen. 49:15). Israelites and Canaanites intermarried and exchanged cultures. Israelites paid their respects to local gods as well as Yahweh at Canaanite shrines; Canaanites revered Yahweh as another saviour. The two peoples were largely merged by Solomon's reign.

But Dtr[1], pressing Josiah's reform of Israelite religion, looked back to a mythical age of purity of the Israelites and the Yahwist cult. He taught that the Israelites slaughtered or drove out the Canaanites before them in the conquest of Canaan. To prove that Shechem had never been anything but a shrine to Yahweh alone, Dtr[1] had Moses command that his laws be read at Mount Ebal (Deut. 11:27-31), and Joshua carry out the command (Josh. 8). Trying to stop priests of other gods from restoring their cults at Shechem and other Canaanite temples, and to protect Solomon's temple financially, Dtr[1] insisted that no altar should be built to Yahweh in competition with the Jerusalem temple. He made concessions to those living far from Jerusalem, but they still had to come to Jerusalem with gifts and sacrifices (Josh. 22; Deut. 12:21, 14:24-26).

Joshua 13-21 describes the tribal territories in David's time. In the original ending of Joshua, Dtr[1] wrote Joshua's farewell speech to preach loyalty to Yahweh (Josh. 23).

Judges. This book represents the confused and haphazard nature of the conquest somewhat more accurately than does Joshua. But Judges is an artificial portrayal of the period when the tribes of Israel were still independent, each ruled by some sort of patriarch, chief, or priest. Dtr[1] created Judges to draw all the peoples of Judah and Samaria into the service of Yahweh alone. He took folk tales of heroes from a book of liberators of the northern kingdom and blended them with historical figures. His heroes were Deborah and Barak, Ehud, Jephthah, Samson, and Gideon.

It did not matter that Deborah and Barak were earlier than the judges. The song of Deborah is a precious glimpse of the conquest, about 1150 BC. It boasted of defeating Canaanites in the plain of Jezreel by attacking in the wet season when iron chariot wheels stuck in mud (Judg. 5:1-31). Ordinarily the Israelites were no match for war-chariots (Judg. 1:19; Josh. 17:16-18; 1 Kings 20:23). Deborah was a most unusual woman for the patriarchal desert folk.

Nor did Dtr[1] realize that Gideon (Jerubaal) and his son Abimelech had Canaanite names. The stories were Canaanite even if the heroes performed Yahweh's missions.

Other heroic "judges" fought Moabites, Ammonites, and Midianites, peoples much like the Israelites who normally only wanted to keep their flocks alive long enough to go back into their winter grazing grounds in the desert, but occasionally turned to raiding the settlements.

Stories about Philistines originated between 1200 and 1000 BC. Philistines came down from Asia Minor and the Aegean looking for a new homeland. Pharaoh Rameses III kept them from entering Egypt, and they settled along the coast from Gaza northward by 1170 BC. They were not Semites, but took the Semitic god Dagon as their protector. The tribe of Dan, settling west of Jerusalem after 1200 BC, memorialized the Philistines in the Samson folk tales.

Dtr[1] wrongly made each judge a ruler of all Israel, whereas a judge was at most the leader of a single tribe. Dtr[1] made the twelve judges rule consecutively to fill out the 480 years from the exodus to Solomon's temple (1 Kings 6:1). Twelve was a mystical number derived from the twelve months of the year

and the constellations of the zodiac. Dtr[1] dug up seven obscure judges to round out his twelve. Othniel was one of
these, brought in to represent the tribe of Judah. Othniel, like
Deborah, belonged to the conquest, not the period of the
judges. Jephthah was the only hero in the list of twelve who
actually was a judge. Samson was a folk hero who made fools
of the Philistines. Today's reader seldom appreciates how
comical and preposterous the stories are, or compares Samson's feats with Paul Bunyan's. Our sense of humor must have
degenerated since the Samson stories were composed!

Samuel and Kings. The large Hebrew book of Kings is divided
into four in the Old Testament: 1, 2 Samuel and 1, 2 Kings.
It begins with the delightful stories of Samuel and Eli his father, and continues through the kings of Israel and Judah. It
ends with Josiah's reign and exile to Babylonia. The promi-
nence of the Shiloh stories and Jeremiah's grief at Shiloh's destruction (Jer. 7:12-14) confirms that he was Dtr[1].

Dtr[1] included three different stories of Saul's becoming king
of the northern tribes. In one story from Gilgal, the people
acclaim him king and seal the acclamation with a communion
sacrifice to Yahweh (1 Sam. 11). In a story from Ramah,
Samuel's home, Yahweh chooses Saul through Samuel the
medium after the people demanded a king (1 Sam. 8; 10:17-
24; 12). In the third story, also from Ramah, Samuel anoints
Saul as king, and when Saul meets a group of ecstatic
prophets, he is seized with the spirit of Yahweh. This passage
provides insight into the prophetic tradition, a movement
that later became important in Kabbalah and Christianity (1
Sam. 9-10:16; 19:20-24). The stories also reflect controversies
in Dtr[1]'s time about the kingship. Kings often became
despots, and some people yearned for the mythical age when
Yahweh ruled directly without the mediary of kings, only
priests. Dtr[1]'s stories and comments showed that Yahweh fa-

vored having a king over the Israelites; Dtr[1], Josiah's advisor, thought that Josiah always did what was right.

Dtr[1] wove together two different stories about the first meeting of Saul and David. The battle between David and Goliath (1 Sam. 17:37-53) comes from both stories. Saul chose David for his armor-carrier and harpist in one story (1 Sam. 16:14-23, 17:1-11) but did not know him in the other (1 Sam. 17:12-30, 17:55-18:5).

As for Goliath's killer, he was Elhanan, not David (2 Sam. 21:19 in the Hebrew version). It is likely that David's poets invented the David and Goliath stories to magnify him in lavish praises *after* he was king. The marvelous description of Goliath in his bronze age armor confirms the theory that the Philistines had come from the Aegean.

Yahweh, changing his mind about Saul, dispatched Samuel to anoint David. The spirit of Yahweh left Saul and settled on David, and an evil spirit settled on Saul (1 Sam. 15:10-16:23). Here Dtr[1] was trying to prove David's righteousness. The original Saul stories may well have accused David of murdering Saul and his sons.

Dtr[1] included the story that David brought into Jerusalem the ark and tablets that came from Shiloh. Dtr[1] probably intended that story to strengthen the authority of the Mosaic priests. The Aaronids must have had their own ark, tablets, and tabernacle, in Jerusalem. Dtr[1] fervently hoped that David's dynasty would last forever; he cited Yahweh's promise that it would (2 Sam. 7). Dtr[1] represented David as loyal to Yahweh, but the real David probably also sacrificed to Canaanite gods at their temples to get their help. Almost everyone did, including Solomon, in that age of superstition.

Dtr[1] cites what appear to be palace records: the book of the annals of Solomon (1 Kings 11:41) and, after the kingdom split, the annals of the kings of Israel and the annals of the kings of Judah. The Elijah and Elisha legends came from the north (1 Kings 17-2 Kings 13).

Dtr[1] judges each king of Judah and Israel on whether he obeyed Yahweh or not. He regards most of the kings of Israel as evil; that was why their reigns and dynasties were so short, and why Israel was destroyed in 722. He regards several of the kings of Judah as good, notably Hezekiah, who destroyed the altars and sanctuaries of the foreign gods and destroyed the bronze snake that Moses had used to heal snakebite (Num. 21:8-9; 2 Kings 18:4). But Yahweh protected Judah regardless of the behavior of its kings, for he had promised David that his descendents would reign forever.

Josiah's grandfather, Manasseh, was wicked in Dtr[1]'s eyes: he had sacrificed his son at Topheth. As we shall see in later chapters, kings sometimes performed human sacrifice to persuade the gods to save them from their enemies. Manasseh may have made his sacrifice to gain the gods' protection from Assyria when she sent a huge army down the coast in 671 BC. Assyria devastated Lower Egypt but spared Judah, probably because Manasseh gave in and sent tribute and erected altars to the Assyrian king and gods. Manasseh "shed much innocent blood." Tradition held that he martyred Isaiah.

Manasseh's son Amon succeeded him in 642 and continued his practices. Amon's servants murdered him after only two years. The "people of the land"—probably Yahwist landowners in Judah—executed the conspirators, then installed the eight-year old Josiah (2 Kings 11:18-20; 14:19-21; 23:30). No doubt Josiah "ruled" with aid of a regency who guided him toward a greater humanism as well as loyalty to Yahweh.

Josiah's Reign

Assyria declined as Scythians invaded from the north, and so Judah could put money into temple repairs. Hilkiah found the D document in the temple and proclaimed it as the true law of Moses. Josiah renewed the covenant with Yahweh, initiated the reform, and sealed the covenant with the passover celebration in honor of Yahweh's aid in the flight across the Red Sea. Dtr[1]—Jeremiah—praised Josiah, "There was no such king before him according to the law of Moses!" (2 Kings 23:25). Zephaniah also praised Josiah's reform, and criticized the earlier kings for not trusting and obeying Yahweh. He attacked the foppish courtiers for deceit and plots, some of which were likely directed against Josiah. He faulted the priests for serving other gods and for other outrages against *torah* (Zeph. 1).

Did Hilkiah and his family create the D document, arrange Amon's death, indoctrinate the young king, and guide the reform of Israelite religion? Perhaps. Jeremiah began advising the king when the latter was twenty-one. Jeremiah was deeply involved in Josiah's reform, for he cited Manasseh's evils (Jer. 3; 7:31-32). But vested interests reversed Josiah's reform after his death.

We will discuss that reversal further in chapter six. First we will see the ancient stories which the writers of the kingdoms of Israel and Judah wrote down (chapter three) and the *torahs* that were written long before Josiah's time (chapters four and five). That will provide a better understanding of the traditions and writings that had been handed down to Hilkiah, the Deuteronomist, and Josiah from the previous generation.

3

The Oldest Writings

Deuteronomy is now the final and climactic book of the Torah. Its central part, the law of Moses that Hilkiah found, guided the nation to sweeping reforms. But surely Genesis, Exodus, Leviticus, and Numbers—or at least materials in them—are older, for Deuteronomy builds upon events described in those books. What is the origin of the first four books of the Torah? To answer that question, we must identify the most ancient writings in the Bible.

The Tradition of Writing

Writing presupposes literacy. The walled cities of Canaan were centers of learning in the bronze age. The great Canaanite empire extended almost to Asia Minor and lasted from 2500 to 1200 BC. Kings had secretaries to write letters and treaties. Recorders kept lists of personnel, historical events, taxes, arms, valuables, and food supplies. Priests wrote magical formulas, hymns, myths, prayers, liturgies. The leisure class reared poets and sages. The elite created schools to prepare their sons to step into their shoes. The archives in the ruins of the great cities of Ugarit and Ebla in the north are revealing much new information about the Canaanite empire. Jerusalem, Ziklag, Gaza, and Hebron were southern outposts of this empire.

The Israelites had a tradition of early relationships with the Jebusites, the Canaanite inhabitants of Jerusalem (Gen. 14:18-

19). The prefix, *Je-*, indicates that Yahweh was their greatest god. Probably the Jebusites had settled in earlier waves from other cities and the desert. The distinction between Israelites and Canaanites was not as sharp as Dtr[1] thought; Canaanites believed that Abraham was their ancestor, too. By Dtr[1]'s time most of the settled peoples of Israel and Judah called themselves Israelites. Ishmaelites and Midianites were still living in the desert.

Opportunities for shepherds to learn to read and write were probably limited to their summers near oases and cities, and occasional meetings with caravans travelling between Egypt and Mesopotamia. When the Israelites settled, those who quickly learned to read and write might have found opportunities in palaces, warehouses, and temples. The Israelites brought a rich oral tradition of their desert life and combined them with Canaanite myths and legends.

The Levites were Israelite shepherds who had been slaves in Egypt, and when they returned to the desert they amazed other tribes with their knowledge of magic from Egypt. The Levites made a living from their mysterious rites. Their sanctuaries were tents where grotesque winged animals guarded a chest containing a covenant with Yahweh. Yahweh hovered invisibly above the chest. The Levites kept records and taught respect for the written word. They were among the last of the Israelites to settle. Those who claimed descent from Moses came into the central hills north of Jerusalem from the Transjordan, while the descendents of Aaron came into Judah from the south. The Levites claimed superior knowledge of Yahweh (their miraculous escape across the Red Sea was only one of many proofs), and so they were less tolerant of other cults than were most peoples.

Writing in David's empire. David, king of Israel and Judah, took Jerusalem by surprise through underground passages (2 Sam. 5:6-10), so he probably took over its palace, temples, and personnel with little resistance. The story of the battle of the kings in the vale of Siddim (Gen. 14) might have come from Jebusite libraries, for there is a resemblance with writings found at Ebla. David extended his territories and influence to Edom, Tyre, Damascus, and the Transjordan through marriage, diplomacy, and war. He had ambassadors, recorders, and scribes (2 Sam. 8:16-17; 20:24-25) and took a census (2 Sam. 24), so he had literate officials who would have demanded schools for their sons.

Dtr[1] had considerable literature to select from in writing the books of Samuel and Kings. He wanted to represent David as obedient to Yahweh to justify his claim that his descendents would rule forever under Yahweh's protection. But Dtr[1] couldn't distinguish bedroom fiction from fact, and had to include the stories that made David a murderer and lecherer. By the time the Chronicler wrote, David had become a saint with shining face and halo. The Chronicler cited annals of King David and reports from seers (1 Chron. 27:24; 9:29-30), but they may have been pious fiction written centuries after David. The Israelites' love of stories blossomed into literature in his reign. Still, no writing has been identified from David's reign with certainty; a good candidate is some history with little embellishment (such as 2 Sam. 5:4-5).

Writing in Solomon's empire. One of David's sons by a Jebusite wife inherited the kingship. Solomon became proverbial for his many wives, wealth, wisdom, military might, and foreign contacts. His magnificent temple was a great center for the priesthood and religious education for centuries. Solomon had recorders and scribes (1 Kings 4:1-4). Solomon "spoke three thousand proverbs" (1 Kings 4:32), and the book of Proverbs is attributed to Solomon. The oldest parts are two collections of independent doublets. The first collection probably came from Solomon's time (Prov. 10-22:16), and it has an appendix (Prov. 22:17-24:34) of more elaborate sayings which, up to Prov. 23:11, resemble Egyptian aphorisms of Solomon's time. The second collection of doublets was written in Hezekiah's reign (Prov. 25-29); its appendix is of uncertain date (Prov. 30-31). The prolog (Prov. 1-9) was written after the exile. Nothing relates the Song of Songs to Solomon, though his "songs were a thousand and five." They are timeless, resembling ancient Egyptian wedding songs as well as more recent Arab love songs. The book of the acts of Solomon (1 Kings 11:41) is unknown.

Writing in the two kingdom period. After Solomon died, Judah acclaimed his son Rehoboam king. But when Rehoboam went to Shechem to be made king of Israel, the people refused to crown him unless he reduced taxes and labor requirements. Rehoboam spurned their demands, so they crowned Jeroboam I. Thereafter, Israel went its separate way.

Israel and Judah were often enemies, often allies, but always rivals, with Israel fearful of Jerusalem's domination.

The following story illustrates the feud between Israel and Judah. Jeroboam had two golden bulls made for the sanctuaries to Yahweh in Beth-El and Dan (1 Kings 12:25-31). But when Josiah stamped out worship of these Canaanite symbols of strength and virility, Mosaic priests blamed Aaron for the practice (Exod. 32:1-35).

Jezebel, King Ahab's Phoenician wife, imposed her fertility cult of Ashtoreth (Ishtar) on Israel and persecuted the priests of Yahweh. The common people loved their men of Yahweh, and the tradition ran deep (1 Sam. 9:7; 10:5; 1 Kings 22:11-28). Elijah had to flee Jezebel's persecution. The Yahwists led a revolt against Jezebel and her priests. The Israelites had tolerated many cults, but after Jezebel's persecutions, Yahweh would never again be just one of the gods.

Jerusalem was a safe place for the kings' archives and temple libraries for three hundred years, for the Dead Sea and desert protected her. David's descendents ruled until the exile. Israel had scribes, priests, sages, and poets who produced records and literature, but much was destroyed in the frequent invasions from the north. Nevertheless, both Judah and Israel produced major writings that form important sections of the Old Testament. As we see below, the writings from the two kingdoms are often parallel, and they are often distinguishable.

Parallel Writings in Israel and Judah

Duplicated psalms. Psalms 1-41 and 51-70 are labelled, "of David." A few psalms in these groups are duplicated: Psalms 14 and 53 are similar; Psalms 40:13-17 and 70 are parallel. Psalm 108 is a combination of Psalms 57:7-11 with 60:5-12.

Why should the psalms be duplicated? Poets and singers in both Israel and Judah wrote psalms for their temple services, and they would exchange them. Eventually the two sets were brought together.

The differences between duplicate psalms are revealing. In the original Hebrew, the letters "YHWH" appear often in Psalms 1-41. "YHWH" was an abbreviation for "Yahweh," but is translated "Lord" in the King James and some other versions.

But Psalms 51-70 usually use "Elohim," which is translated "God."

Parallel stories in Genesis. The Hagar and Ishmael story is told twice, though with variations. *The first version uses the name Yahweh:*

Sarai was infertile, so she gave her slave Hagar to Abram to bear his child. Hagar conceived. Then Sarai felt she had lost Hagar's respect, so she abused Hagar until she ran away into the desert. Yahweh's angel found her by a fountain. After hearing that she had been driven away, he told her to go back. He said she would have a son who would be called

Ishmael, for "Yahweh has heard your affliction." Ishmael would give rise to a great warlike tribe (Gen. 16:1-15).

The second version speaks of Elohim. Several details show that it was originally the same story, though it has been made into a sequel taking place several years later:

Sarah miraculously bore a son, Isaac. After he was weaned, Sarah asked Abraham to drive Hagar and her son away. Elohim assured Abraham that both Isaac and "the son of the bondswoman" would father great nations. Elohim heard the voice of the abandoned boy, and Elohim's angel told Hagar so, though the boy's name is not stated. Elohim promised that he would sire a great nation. Elohim opened Hagar's eyes, and she saw a well where she could draw water. Elohim was with the lad, who became an archer of the wilderness (Gen. 21:1-21).

The J and E Writers

Writings that predominantly use the name Yahweh are usually about Judah. They are called J from the German spelling, Jahweh, for Yahweh. The unknown writers of the J document are called the Jahwist or Yahwist. By happy circumstance, Judah and Jerusalem begin with J. So J = Jahwist = Judah.

Writings that mostly use the Canaanite title, Elohim, are usually about Ephraim in the northern kingdom of Israel, so they were probably composed there. The writers are collectively called the Elohist, and their writings, E. They were Yahwists in the broad sense in that they worshipped Yahweh, but usually by the Canaanite title. Again, E = Elohist = Ephraim = Israel.

The differences between the J and E documents are numerous, involving places, names, dialect, and such-like which are obvious to the Bible scholar in Hebrew. J is a desert herdsman; E, a farmer-herdsman. When J climbs Sinai, E ascends Horeb. Where J meets Ishmaelites, E sees Midianites.

Thus, Psalms 51-70 are Elohist, and they were sung in the several sanctuaries of Israel. The Yahwist Psalms 1-41 were sung in Solomon's temple or other shrines in Judah.

The book of Psalms includes other collections. Two are labelled "sons of Korah" (E, Ps. 42-49, J, Ps. 84-85, 87-88); another, "of Asaph" (E, Ps. 50, 73-83). Psalm 72 bears a subscript, "End of the prayers of David," indicating that it came at the end of a collection. Psalm 84 on are Yahwist except for 108.

The Israelites who entered Canaan from the desert probably did not think that their god of the wilderness was the same as Elohim, the greatest god of the walled cities. Their rituals and myths were probably different from Canaanite, but merged as the people and their cultures intermingled. Ultimately Elohim and Yahweh were declared one and the same. Why did E use the name Elohim for Yahweh who had led them out of the desert? Perhaps Elohim seemed more respectful or sophisticated, but the priests of Jerusalem and the rustic prophets of both kingdoms preferred Yahweh's unpolished name from the wilderness.

Other J and E Stories in Genesis

Let us look at some more J and E stories to understand how the Yahwist and Elohist thought.

Gossip and Legends. Genesis is full of delicious gossip about personal lives. There are quarrels, conspiracies, feuds, murders, heroics, love affairs, betrothals, children, comedies, tragedies. They were stories told at wells and around campfires.

The following story is so juicy that it turns up in three versions. After Abram arrived in Canaan, he went on to

Egypt. On the way, Abram and Sarai agreed to tell the Egyptians that she was Abram's sister, out of fear. When the Egyptians took Sarai to the Pharaoh, he kept her. But Yahweh plagued Pharaoh until he realized his error and let her go (J, Gen. 12:10-20). Abraham had the same misunderstanding with Abimelech (E, Gen. 20). So did Isaac and Rebekah (J, Gen. 26:6-10).

Clever Jacob cheated his father-in-law Laban out of his flocks (Gen. 30:25-31:18). Rachel stole Laban's idols and sat on them while he searched her tent (J, Gen. 31:18-35).

The Elohist's "fear of Isaac" and "terror of Elohim," J's "horror of great darkness," the smoking furnace, and "burning lamp passing between bloody pieces of flesh"—these ghost stories frightened and thrilled children around glowing embers in the dark of the moon (Gen. 31:42, 35:5, 15:12,17). But they may point to important traditions: for example, walking between halves of carcasses (Gen. 15:8-17) sealed contracts in Sumer in 2000 BC.

Man-like gods. In the dawning of civilization, gods walked upon the earth, and animals talked to people. Gods resembled men in form and thought processes. Thus Yahweh, like the titan Prometheus, shaped man from earth with his hands. Yahweh breathed life into his nostrils (with mouth and lungs), had a garden (gods had to eat), and walked in it. He did not know where Adam was hiding (Gen. 2:7, 3:8-9).

Gods descended to earth long ago; they loved young women and sired a race of giants (J, Gen. 6:2-4). Stars were gods, the host of heaven. The Milky Way was their stairway; people saw them travelling up and down on it from afar. Jacob saw them up close, for he slept at an ancient Canaanite holy place which he named Beth-El, the house of God (E, Gen. 28:12).

Jacob wrestled with a man. Neither was winning. The stranger magically shrank a muscle in Jacob's thigh, so Jacob knew he was a god. Jacob would not let him escape as dawn approached (gods have to get back before sunrise), and thus Jacob forced him to bless him (E, Gen. 32:24-32). Perhaps the story arose like this: Some hitherto-invincible man came home, lamed for life. Refusing to admit that another man could beat him, he bragged of fighting a being greater than any man. His injuries proved it. At least he made the god tell his name and used it to exact a promise before letting him go. (One who knows a god's name can make him do favors. A pious editor changed the god's name to Elohim.) It has been suggested that the hero reenacted his fight with a dance that survived for generations.

Why things are. Many stories tell why things are the way they are. The Hagar story explained why Ishmaelites resembled Israelites but stayed in the desert, and how they got their name. It also explained why the well was called the well of vision or sight, Lahai Roi: Hagar saw a god and called him El Roi, god of vision (J, Gen. 16:13). An editor thought it meant that she was not blinded when she saw him, so he added verse 14, for seeing a god caused blindness or death (E, Exod. 33:20.) But in E, Elohim remained invisible when he opened Hagar's eyes. She saw a well, so it became the well of vision (Gen. 21:19).

The Israelites did not eat the inside of the thigh, nor do some orthodox Jews today. The story that a god touched Jacob's thigh and lamed him (E, Gen. 32:24-32) explained both the custom and the meagerness of flesh there.

We learn why snakes have no legs, why they are poisonous, why childbirth is painful, why life is so hard, why women serve men, why thorns and thistles thrive, why we have to work, why we wear clothes, why we are like the gods in knowledge, why we should not ask so many questions, and why, unlike the gods, we must die (J, Gen. 3:1-19). These situations remind us of myths of other peoples. In J, a snake talked Eve into stealing fruit from the tree of knowledge of good and evil. In Greek mythology, the titan Prometheus wanted to put man above all other animals, so he gave him fire stolen from the chariot of the sun. But that divine gift elevated him excessively above other animals, and made him like the gods in knowledge.

Gods in particular places. Some stories showed the gods living in definite localities. The god who spoke to Hagar lived at the well in the original story. Wells and oases saved lives in the desert, and allowed grazing and planting. But if someone angered him, the god might dry up the source or pollute it with disease. Editors changed the god's name to Yahweh or Elohim.

Angels entertained unawares. A common myth among ancient folk was that gods visit the earth to check up on people. One never knows when visitors are gods in disguise, so be kind to strangers. In the homeland of the tale of the aged Philemon and his wife Baucis, the natives mistook Paul and Barnabas for Zeus and Hermes (Acts 14:12). Hospitality is legendary among desert people; bedouins still have rigid customs about receiving visitors. Abraham saw three men walking toward his tent. He ran out to greet them and invite them in. He washed their feet, and Sarah fed them. In gratitude for the aged couple's hospitality, one of the gods promised them a son. Sarah laughed, but denied it when the god chided her. It is not clear that Yahweh was one of the three gods; an editor added the invisible YHWH to the story (J, Gen. 18:1-15). For more on laughter, see Gen. 17:17, 21:6.

Yahweh said that he was on his way to Sodom and Gomorrah. The kindly Abraham talked him into sparing the cities if he found ten righteous people (J, Gen. 18:23-33). The grim landscape around the Dead Sea inspired the story of destruction, for rock-salt pinnacles looked like tents and people in robes.

Patriarchs' idols. Rachel stole Laban's household gods (p. 36). At Luz, a Canaanite shrine, Jacob erected a stone pillar and poured wine and oil on it. He renamed the place Beth-El, "house of God" (E, Gen. 35:6-15; J, Gen. 28:16-19).

Abraham planted *asherah* at Beersheba, an oasis where his flocks could survive the summer (Gen. 21:33-34). *Asherah? Asherah* means a grove or tree. The same word was used when Josiah destroyed groves or trees (2 Kings 23:4, 6, 14-15). Why would Josiah cut down trees? Actually Josiah destroyed idols of Ashtoreth (Ishtar), the Semitic Venus! Ideas about the supernatural changed over time, and editors often removed or reworded offensive material in older writings. So where the Elohist praised Abraham's devotion to Ashtoreth, a priest of Yahweh replaced *Ashtoreth* with *asherah*, grove or tree, so as not to admit that Abraham worshipped other gods.

Ancestors as gods. "Fear of Isaac" (Gen. 31:42) suggests that Isaac's spirit was still around.

Explanations of names. We may never have wondered how Peniel got its name, but the Israelites did. Or at least they enjoyed hearing that it was where Jacob looked a god in the face (Gen. 32:30). Israel got its name because Jacob, its mythical ancestor, prevailed against a god (Gen. 32:28). Mahanaim was so called because Jacob saw many gods there (Gen. 32:1-2). El 'Olan at Beersheba (E, Gen. 21:33*ff*) could mean well of the seven (sheep), or well of the oath (J, Gen. 26:33). Isaac meant laughter; Ishmael meant God heard. Experts in Hebrew and related languages recognize these stories as popular but usually wrong attempts to explain names whose true meanings were long forgotten.

Origins of tribes and nations. Jacob (Israel) was the father of twelve sons, thus of the twelve mythical tribes of Israelites. His blessing was a song that J wrote down (Gen. 49:1-14). Jacob's brother Esau fathered the tribe of Edom, which became a kingdom. Ishmael was the father of the Arabs;

Abraham, of all the peoples from the Euphrates to the border of Egypt. Such explanations are simplistic on a large scale, but they were based on facts of life of desert tribes. Tribes were patrilineal, tracing themselves to a male ancestor as though mothers counted for nothing. The patriarch ruled the tribe and gave it his name. He had children by concubines and by his many wives, who were usually half-sisters and cousins. His sons shared in ruling the tribe. Successful tribes grew and divided, and related tribes cooperated in defense. Some fell on hard luck, dwindled and died out or merged with others. Patriarchy, patrilineality, patronymy, and inbreeding continued among the Israelites after settlement, along with intermarriage with Canaanites.

Poetry. Poetry and song turn up everywhere in the Bible. The New Jerusalem Bible sets off verse to make it easy to distinguish from prose. Poetry and song are passed on for generations in preliterate societies (oral tradition). J and E recorded considerable ancient poetry. The first J example is as follows: This is now bone of my bones/ and flesh of my flesh/ She is to be called woman/ because she was taken out of man (Gen. 2:23). Hebrew poetry commonly consists of couplets in which two lines are parallel in some way. In this example the first two lines are parallel, and the second two are parallel.

J and E Stories in Exodus

J and E both had Moses stories and laws, and they are now in Exodus and Numbers.

Moses in the basket. A thousand years before Moses, this J story was told about Sargon of Akkad on the Euphrates (Exod. 1:22-2:10).

Yahweh or Elohim calls Moses. *The J story:* Moses fled from Pharaoh and lived in Midian. He married Zipporah, daughter of Reuel, a priest of Midian. The king of Egypt died (Exod.

1:15-23a). The angel of Yahweh spoke to Moses out of a burning bush, and when Yahweh saw him turn to look (Exod. 3:2-4a) he told Moses to take off his sandals for it was holy ground (Exod. 3:5). Yahweh promised to lead the Israelites out of their misery to the land of Canaan (Exod. 3:7-8). Yahweh gave Moses magical powers. His brother Aaron would be spokesman—this shows the Yahwist's bias. Yahweh would tell both what to say (Exod. 4:1-17). Yahweh told Moses to leave Midian and return to Egypt. Moses put his wife and sons on an ass and returned to Egypt (Exod. 4:19-20a). Yahweh met Moses and tried to kill him. (!) Zipporah saved Moses by throwing a foreskin at the god's genitals (Exod. 4:21b, 22-31). (The last part of the story was censored, but what was deleted? that Moses was not circumcised? or his son? that Moses wrestled with Yahweh and defeated him?)

The E story: Moses tended sheep in Midian, Arabia (Exod. 3:1; an editor added Horeb to place it in Sinai). Elohim called him (Exod. 3:4b). Elohim said, I am Elohim of your father, Abraham, Isaac, and Jacob. Moses hid his face for fear of death (Exod. 3:6). Elohim promised to lead them out of Egypt and to Canaan; Moses protested and asked his name. Elohim told his name: I AM THAT I AM, Yahweh Elohim of his fathers, etc. (Exod. 4:9-15). Moses begged his father-in-law (Jethro in this E version) for permission to return to Egypt. Jethro sent him in peace (Exod. 4:18). Moses took the magician's rod that Elohim give him (4:20b).

Moses' father-in-law, Reuel or Jethro, was also Hobab the Kenite (Josh. 1:16, Judg. 4:11). An editor tried to clarify the disparity (Num. 10:29).

The plagues. J and E each listed several plagues. Scholars disagree on the exact division. By one count, J listed seven (plagues 1, 2, 4, 5, 7, 8, 10), while E had five (1, 7, 8, 9, 10). Plagues 3 and 6 came from a later writer.

The passover. *The J version:* Moses told the elders to kill a lamb for the passover, dip hyssop in its blood to sprinkle the lintel and sideposts of each house. None shall go out until morning (Exod. 12:21-23).

The E version: They held a passover sacrifice, borrowed valuables, fled by night, and baked unleavened bread (Exod. 12:24-27, 29-36, 38-39). All firstborn were Yahweh's; he seems to demand human sacrifice, then demands a substitute instead (Exod. 13:1-2, 11-13, 14-16).

Crossing of the Red Sea. *This is the J version:* The king of Egypt pursued Israel with six hundred chariots (Exod. 14:5-7) and marched after them (Exod. 14:10b). Moses told his people, Fear not, stand still, and watch Yahweh fight your battle (Exod. 14:13-14). The pillar of the cloud went from before their face, and stood behind them (Exod. 14:19b) and gave light by night (Exod. 14:20b). All night Yahweh caused a strong east wind to drive back the sea (Exod. 14:21b). In the morning Yahweh looked at the Egyptian army through the pillar of fire and the cloud, and worried them (Exod. 14:24), so they tried to flee (Exod. 14:25b). But Yahweh overthrew the Egyptians in the midst of the sea (Exod. 14:27b). Thus Yahweh saved Israel. So the people feared and believed Yahweh and his servant Moses (Exod. 14:30-31). Then J inserted an ancient song of the sea (Exod. 15:1-18).

This is the Elohist's story: When Pharaoh let the people go, Elohim led them through the wilderness of the Red Sea, and they left Egypt without harm. Moses brought Joseph's bones (Exod. 13:17-19) as requested (E, Gen. 49:24-26). The people complained that they should have stayed in Egypt rather than die in the wilderness (Exod. 14:11-12). The angel of Elohim went before the camp of Israel, then went behind them (Exod. 14:19a) to separate the Egyptian and Israelite camps (Exod. 14:20a). He took off the Egyptians' chariot wheels (Exod. 14:25). E preserved a precious bit of song as follows. Miriam the sister of Aaron took a timbrel in her hand, and all the women went dancing out after her with timbrels. And Miriam answered them, Sing to Yahweh, for he has triumphed gloriously/ he has thrown the horse and his rider into the sea (Exod. 14:20-21).

Covenants with Yahweh and Elohim. Yahweh gave the Israelites a covenant (Exod. 19-24; 34). The J and E stories are intertwined with a later one, creating utter confusion. Each is rather simple if separated out, as follows:

The J story: Moses sanctified the people for three days, then Yahweh descended on Sinai (Exod. 19:10-15). Yahweh was a god of smoke and fire like a volcano (Midian, southeast of the Dead Sea, in Arabia, had active volcanoes; Exod. 19:18). Moses went up, then came back to tell them to keep away (Exod. 19:20-25). Yahweh told Moses to prepare two stone tablets (Exod. 34:1a). Moses brought them up. Yahweh dictated an early version of ten commandments, and Moses wrote them on the tablets: no other gods; no idols; observe feast of unleavened bread; offer the firstborn to Yahweh; rest on the sabbath; observe feast of weeks (firstfruits) and feast of ingathering (Sukkot); assemble before Yahweh three times a year; offer no blood with leaven, nor leave passover to morning; bring first of firstfruits to house of Yahweh; never boil a kid in its mother's milk (a Canaanite ritual). Moses stayed on the mount forty days (Exod. 34:2-28). Moses wrote Yahweh's words on tablets and read them to the people. They sealed the covenant with one voice, with sacrifices and sprinkling of blood (Exod. 24:3-8).

This is the Elohist's story: Elohim appeared on the mountain (like a thunderstorm moving into the central hills of Israel from the Mediterranean; Exod. 19:2b-9, 16b-17, 19; 20:18-21). Yahweh gave Moses a long list of instructions, beginning, Tell the children of Israel, You have seen that I have talked with you from heaven (Exod. 20:22). He forbade idolatry

(Exod. 20:23). Immediately follows a long section thought to have originally been a separate Elohist document (Exod. 20:24-23:9). It is wrongly called "the book of the covenant:" it has no list of promises and curses. It first authorizes many altars (Exod. 20:24-26) which D later forbade, and Josiah destroyed. Then follow many ancient laws from the farming and pastoral society including fair treatment of Hebrew slaves, polygamy, homicide, protection from vengeance, and remedies for injuries (Exod. 21:1-22). Then laws resembling Hammurabi's code, 1750 BC (Exod. 21:23-25) The book of the covenant ends at 23:9, but still more laws follow. Yahweh would bring the Israelites into Canaan (Exod. 23:23-33). Some of the instructions above resemble J's ten commandments, but they have not been separated out.

Finally, Yahweh called Moses to come up with Aaron, Nodab, Abihu, and seventy elders (Exod. 24:1).

Now E's story forks in two alternative sequels which might have been written in different temples in Israel. The first resembles a vision from the ecstatic prophetic tradition: Moses, Aaron, and the elders went up and saw Elohim standing on the sapphire firmament. They ate and drank (Exod. 24:9-11).

The second sequel goes as follows: Yahweh called Moses up to receive stone tablets, written commandments, and a law (Exod. 24:2, 12-15). Moses stayed forty days (Exod. 14:18b). He came down, saw Aaron's golden calves, broke the stone tablets that Elohim had inscribed, and talked to Yahweh in the tabernacle (Exod. 32-33). We never find out what was written on the stone tablets.

J and E in Numbers

The J story: The Israelites begin the journey from Sinai with the ark and commandments (Num. 10:29-36). Moses sends spies to Canaan who report that it would be hard to conquer;

there were giants (Num. 13:17*ff*). The people wept that night (Num. 14:1b), wanting to return to Egypt (Num. 14:4). That angered Yahweh; he wanted to kill the Israelites, but Moses pointed out that that would lower his stature among the nations. Caleb would go into Canaan (Num. 14:11-25). Amalekites and Canaanites killed disobedient Israelites (Num. 14:39-45). The ground swallowed Dathan and Abiram when they defied Moses' command to go up to Canaan (Num. 16:1b-2a, 12-14, 25-26, 27b-32a, 33-34). Edom repulsed them (Num. 20:14-21). The Israelites fought Canaanites, Amorites, and Bashanites (Num. 21:1-3, 21-35). Israelites who worshipped other gods were killed (Num. 25:1-5).

The Elohist's story: The Israelites were hungry and wanted to go back to Egypt. Yahwe provided manna and quails. Joshua spoke against ecstatic prophets; Moses defended them. Aaron and Miriam angered Yahweh for slander against Moses (Num. 11-12). The people complained, so Yahweh sent serpents, but Moses provided a magical bronze serpent to heal snakebite (Num. 21:4b-9). The parable of Balak and Balaam taught loyalty to Yahweh (Num. 22:2-24:25). East of the Jordan at Jericho, Moses climbed Mount Nebo and Pisgah to survey Canaan; then he died. That was the original ending of E's portion of Numbers. Dtr[1] transferred it to Deuteronomy (Deut. 34:1-6) to form a close along with his own praise of Moses (Deut. 34:10-12).

So these are the writings of ancient Israel and Judah, recorded before 722 BC when Israel was destroyed. Some of them reach back into the oral traditions. The song of Miriam and the song of the sea go back to some memory of the escape from Egypt; the song of Deborah, which Dtr[1] placed in Judges, goes back to the conquest. Rhyme and rhythm enabled bards and storytellers to transmit their lyrics with remarkable fidelity, even to details that no one understands any more.

Once written, the story changes little except for cause. But J could not know that Abraham did not have camels (despite Gen. 24), since camels were domesticated three hundred years after Abraham. Nor could E know that Abraham lived six hundred years before the Philistines came to Palestine (despite Gen. 21:32). Those stories are precious even if anachronistic. The Yahwist and Elohist collected these tales from the old storytellers, perhaps for their intrinsic interest, maybe to enliven schoolwork. They did not make them up or change them much; they were faithful to the storyteller, the heroes, and the gods.

We may speculate that writing could have begun soon after the conquest. J wrote some sort of *torah* in Judah, possibly beginning in David's reign. It continued in Solomon's temple and palace, and the year 850 BC is often suggested for its completion. The year 750 BC is suggested for completion of the Elohist's writings.

The J writings included the creation of man, the garden of Eden, Noah. The J and E writings included the patriarchs, Moses stories, the laws, the wanderings in the desert, many of the Psalms, and materials that Dtr[1] included in Joshua, Judges, and Samuel. As we shall see, two more centuries passed before J and E writings were incorporated into the present books of Genesis, Exodus, and Numbers. Much happened that will require the next four chapters.

4

The Prophets,
and the JE Torah

We go back to the two kingdom era and Jezebel's rule over Israel. Jezebel's tyranny and Ashtoreth priesthood provoked a Yahwist revolution that ended in 814 BC with Jehu's slaughter of Jezebel's family. King Jehu destroyed the shrines to Canaanite gods. Nevertheless, Dtr[1] faulted Jehu for maintaining "Jeroboam's sin," which was in this case the worship of the golden bulls (2 Kings 10:29), which Dtr[1] called "calves" out of contempt. The Mosaic priests had adopted the bull, Canaanite symbol of virility and power, as a pedestal in place of the ark of the covenant. Yahweh hovered invisibly over the bull, but of course many worshipped the bull.

In Jehu's reign, Israel's economy and power declined, and Syria encroached on her borders. The decline ended after 783 BC when Jehu's great-grandson Jeroboam II took over and restored Israel's former boundaries. A great diplomat, Jeroboam II developed trade and alliances with his neighbors. His was an age of prosperity and peace.

Amos

But the Yahwists criticized Jeroboam II for keeping the golden bulls (2 Kings 14:24). And they faulted Israel's prosperity. About 760, Amos, a shepherd, came up from Judah and discovered evil in the wealth of the few when so many people remained in poverty. He accused the rich of cheating and oppressing the poor. He condemned the shrines of Beth-El, Samaria, Gilgal, and Dan, which Yahweh had to share with Canaanite gods. He said that insincere rituals and sacrifices disgusted Yahweh. He predicted that Yahweh would punish Israel by destruction, slaughter, and exile. His concern was real, for Assyria was crushing nations and scattering their populations. Amaziah, priest of Beth-El, accused Amos of fomenting rebellion and sent him home.

Hosea

Jeroboam II had his critics at home. He formed a coalition with Syria to keep Assyria from pushing west. But Hosea derided Jeroboam's alliances, pleading for trust in Yahweh alone and warning of punishment for disobedience. On the other hand, Hosea ridiculed the Yahwist fanatics who plotted to overthrow their king.

Hosea wrote about 750 BC, and Jeroboam II died six years later. His son Zachariah took over, and the anarchy which Amos and Hosea had feared, now began. Zachariah was killed within six months by Shallum. Menahem usurped the throne a month later. He paid tribute to Assyria and reigned ten years.

Isaiah and Micah

In Judah, Isaiah came to the court in 740 BC, the last year of Uzziah's (Azariah's) reign. Isaiah had considerable power; he was probably related to the kings. His career extended through the reigns of Jotham, Ahaz, and Hezekiah. Micah joined Isaiah in Jotham's reign. Ahaz became king of Judah in 736.

Pekah, usurper to the throne of Israel, demanded that Ahaz join the Israel-Syria coalition against Assyria. But Isaiah warned Ahaz that Assyria would destroy the coalition before it gathered strength. Isaiah urged strict neutrality and careful loyalty to Yahweh for his protection. When Israel-Syria threatened to replace Ahaz with a puppet, Ahaz was ready to give in and join the alliance.

But Isaiah argued, "The coalition can't last." He put his arms around his pregnant wife. "Look, I will name my son, 'Immanuel, God is with us,' and Assyria will smash the alliance before Immanuel knows right from wrong. Never forget that Yahweh is on *our* side, not theirs."

Pekah threatened war if Judah did not join him. Ahaz was frightened and wanted to capitulate. Angry with Ahaz' nervousness, Isaiah retorted, "Go right ahead! I won't call my son 'Immanuel' but 'Quick booty,' because he will be just one more slave if we provoke Assyria!" He urged Ahaz to keep faith with Yahweh and destroy every idol in the nation. Micah supported Isaiah wholeheartedly.

Israel-Syria threw a siege around Jerusalem. Ahaz sent gifts to Tiglath-Pileser, king of Assyria, along with a plea for aid. Tiglath-Pileser obliged by capturing Damascus. Pekah lifted his siege, and Tiglath-Pileser replaced him with Hoshea.

In 734 BC, Ahaz went to Damascus to prostrate himself before Tiglath-Pileser and make a treaty with him. The vassal Ahaz admired Tiglath-Pileser's bronze altar with its idol of Shamash in his chariot drawn by white horses. Ahaz ordered Urijah the priest to make a duplicate for Solomon's temple, in place of Yahweh's altar. So the nation of Judah sacrificed to Tiglath-Pileser, incarnation of Shamash the sun god, greatest god of the nations. That is what Dtr[1] said (2 Kings 16), and he said much more: *"Ahaz walked in the way of the kings of Israel, yea, and made his son pass through the fire..."* (2 Kings 16:3). Ahaz sacrificed his son! And so had the kings of Israel!

When did Ahaz do it? Probably in the desperation of Pekah's siege. What did Isaiah think about child sacrifice, since he was Ahaz' advisor? He did not say. Apparently many kings practiced it in times of dire need, to enlist the ruling god's help. Dtr[1] exposed the custom with two explicit examples. The first was Jephthah's sacrifice of his daughter to Yahweh (Judg. 11:29-40). It illustrated slavish obedience to Yahweh's will. In the second example, the king of Moab sacrificed his son in full view, when the armies of Israel, Judah, and Edom were about to take his city. The attackers gave up the siege, because the god of Moab would surely defeat them after the sacrifice of the king's dearest possession (2 Kings 3:27).

The portions of the book of Isaiah that are regarded as genuinely his are scattered among additions from his admirers: Is.1:5-24; 9:7-21; 10:1-4; 11:1-9; 14:24-32; 17:1-6, 12-14; 20; 22:1-14; 28-32. It is uncertain whether the ecstatic visions of Yahweh on his throne in heaven (Is. 6) were Isaiah's own.

Assyria Destroys Israel

Hoshea, king of Israel and vassal of Assyria, made an alliance with Egypt in 724. Accordingly, Assyria invaded Israel and laid siege to the city of Samaria. Samaria fell in 722. During the invasion, refugees flooded into Jerusalem for the protection of her great walls. The refugees must have had a great effect on Jerusalem. The Mosaic priests among them probably demanded a share of prerogative and cash flow in

Solomon's temple. Their law was "directly" from Moses to back up their claim to authority. The two groups of priests must often have clashed head-on.

Assyria enslaved the people who remained in Israel and drove them to her other territories to settle. Israel was no more; few ever returned. The "ten lost tribes of Israel" melded with the natives of their new homes. Assyria repopulated the land of Israel with captives from other nations. The land of Israel was known as Samaria from that time on. Even though the strangers added Yahweh, god of the land, to their pantheon, the people of Judah never accepted them as Israelites: they were Samaritans. Assyria defeated the Egyptian army below Gaza but did not trouble her vassal Ahaz.

King Hezekiah of Judah

Ahaz died in 716, and Hezekiah succeeded him. When Hezekiah refused to continue tribute to Assyria, Sennacherib the king of Assyria brought a massive army and destroyed the great fortress of Lachish and other cities of Judah. But his siege of Jerusalem in 701 BC was a stand-off: he could not breach the walls, but he did force Hezekiah to pay a large ransom (2 Kings 18:13-16). The miraculous victory (2 Kings 18:17-20:19) was pious fiction written by Isaiah's disciples.

Hezekiah's reign was an era of reform, for he destroyed many altars and removed cult objects from Solomon's temple. It is intriguing to speculate on the politics of the reform, and on Isaiah's role. Who had Moses' bronze snake removed from the temple? (2 Kings 18:4). Probably the Aaronid priests, for they had the power, and the snake was a cult object of the Mosaic priests (E, Num. 21:4b-9).

The JE Document and the JE Editor

An unknown writer valued the literature of both Israel and Judah. He combined and harmonized them to provide a fuller, more authoritative story, incidentally preserving both literatures for us. He was pious, but had a sense of humor. He is the JE editor, or JE. We can see his work in much of Genesis and Exodus, and also in Numbers.

Four examples of JE's art: 1. The J and E versions of the Hagar story were different enough to allow Hagar to be sent into the desert twice. The J version, with child still unborn, was Hagar's first ouster. The E version became her second expulsion, but the young boy was apparently still nameless! JE was faithful to his material, even letting repetitions and small inconsistencies remain.

2. This is the sacrifice of Isaac at Moriah (Gen. 22:1-19). Yes, Abraham sacrificed Isaac in the original E story, for he returned alone (v. 19), and the Elohist never again mentioned Isaac. JE inserted the J verses (11-16a) to provide Abraham with a ram. If those verses are removed, we have a complete E story of Isaac's sacrifice told to exemplify absolute submission to God's will. A similar story extolling obedience to the god has been reported from ancient Sumer. Some Israelites took the story literally and sacrificed their sons to please Yahweh or other gods. JE made the story more humane a hundred years before Josiah put a stop to child sacrifice. Society's regard for children is slow to develop, for child labor laws were enacted only yesterday; millions are abused or neglected, and health care and education are seldom as good as they could be.

3. In the third example, JE created a more complete story about Jacob at Beth-El by cutting both the E and J versions into three pieces and interlacing them. **The J version is in bold:**

Jacob left Beersheba for Haran, and at nightfall stayed at a certain place. He used stones for pillows, and as he slept, he dreamed about a ladder reaching from the earth to heaven, and angels of Elohim went up and down on it. **Yahweh stood above and told Jacob who he was. He promised to look after him and to give the land to his descendents. Jacob woke and said, Yahweh is here, and I didn't know.** He was afraid and said, How awesome is this place! It is Elohim's house, and the gate to heaven. He rose early and set up his pillow-stone as an idol and poured oil on it. **He named the place Beth-El, though the city was originally called Luz.** Jacob vowed, If Elohim will be with me and protect me here, and provide bread and clothing so that I return to my father's house in peace, Yahweh will be my god, and the stone that I erected as an idol will be Elohim's house, and I will give you a tenth of all that you give me (Gen. 28:10-22).

4. JE smoothed the rough edges in the following example, though amusing inconsistencies remain. **The J version is in bold.** *The italicized phrase below was common to both versions and had two different meanings.*

[Joseph's brothers said,] **Here comes Joseph the dreamer. Let us kill him, throw him into a pit, and blame it on a wild animal.** Reuben heard them and took Joseph away from them (intending to take him back to his father) saying, Let us not kill him, but abandon him in this pit in the wilderness. **When Joseph had come to his brothers, they stripped him of his coat of many colors,** and they put him in the pit. They sat down to eat, and when **they looked up, they saw a group of**

Ishmaelites from Gilead with camels loaded with spices for Egypt. Judah said, What profit is it to kill our brother? Let us sell him to the Ishmaelites. His brothers agreed. Then Midianite merchants came by, and *they took Joseph out of the pit* and sold him to the Ishmaelites for twenty pieces of silver, and the Ishmaelites took him to Egypt. Reuben came back to the pit for Joseph, but he was gone, so he tore his clothes in grief. They killed a goat kid, and dipped Joseph's coat in its blood, and took it to their father. He mourned for Joseph. And the Midianites sold Joseph to Potiphar in Egypt (Gen. 37:19-36)... And Joseph was brought to Egypt, and Potiphar bought him from the Ishmaelites (Gen. 39:1).

So the Midianites found Joseph and sold him to the Ishmaelites, then sold him again to Potiphar, and the Ishmaelites sold him to Potiphar!

More important, Reuben was the hero in the E story, for he hid Joseph from his murderous brothers. Judah was the hero in the J story, selling him to the Ishmaelites to get him away from his cutthroat brothers. Reuben and Judah were tribes of the rivalrous Israel and Judah respectively.

JE respected the written word but was not enslaved to it. He changed the meaning of the Isaac story. He twitted the rivalrous priests of the north and south with the paradoxes that he created with his artful snipping and pasting. His classroom rang with the laughter of young students. JE was kind and had a healthy sense of humor.

The JE Torah

Genesis stories: creation and the patriarchs. JE's torah began, "The day that Yahweh Elohim made the earth and the heavens..." (Gen. 2:4b). Elohist material does not appear until Gen. 20; thereafter J and E alternate, either intimately interwoven, or in whole chapters or larger sections. Those are stories of Abraham and his descendents.

That Elohist writings do not appear until Gen. 20 suggests that JE was biased for the J version. But if he used Elohist stories from Gen. 20 on, why not for the creation of Adam and Eve, the garden, Cain and Abel, Noah? Were they too different, or too similar, therefore repetitious? Could the compound name, Yahweh Elohim, Lord God, (Gen. 2-3) acknowledge parallel J and E stories?

JE's torah contained most of the present book of Genesis, but not the material in chapters 1, 5, 17, 23, and many other sections large and small, which, as we shall see, were added centuries later.

Exodus: the Moses stories. JE continues with J's afflictions of the Israelites, E's midwives, J's Moses in the basket, the burning bush, etc. (most of Exod. 1:8-6:1). The following section (Exodus 6:2-7:13) was inserted later; we will meet it in the next chapter. JE listed eight plagues; he did not know the third and sixth (most of Exod. 7:14-11:8). JE combined the J and E versions of the flight (most of Exod. 12:21-15:26).

JE combined the J and E stories of the covenant: Moses brought tablets and many regulations from Horeb, found the golden calf (blamed on Aaron!), and broke the tablets (Exod. 17:2-19:25, 20:18-24:18, 32:1-33:23). JE explained that Yahweh wanted to write on new tablets the same words as on the first (Exod. 34:1). So Moses brought new tablets to receive J's ten commandments (Exod. 32:2-34:28). The breaking of the tablets was probably not just because two stories provided two sets of tablets; J's set was probably in Solomon's temple, but E's set may have been destroyed to hide what was in them. Dtr[1] retold JE's story (Deut. 9:8-10:5) but listed a later version of the ten commandments (Deut. 5:1-21). JE did not include Exodus 25-31, 34:29-40:38.

Numbers: Sinai to Transjordan. JE's story was woven within Num. 10:29-25:5. JE's Numbers ended with E's account of Moses' survey of Canaan, death, and burial at Mount Pisgah. That ending is no longer in Numbers because Dtr[1] moved it to Deut. 34:1-6.

So JE's torah consisted of most of the material in today's book of Genesis, about half of Exodus, and less than half of Numbers. The JE torah may have fit within two scrolls. It included the creation of man, the garden, the patriarchs, Moses' laws, and his leadership to the edge of the promised land. Leviticus and Deuteronomy did not exist at this point.

JE's audacious work was to provoke a harsh reply.

5

The Priestly Code

The appearance of the JE torah in Solomon's temple exacerbated animosities. After all, it was the Aaronid priests' temple, and who were these refugees from the north to insult Aaron with their tale of the golden calf and many other outrages? Why didn't they go home? The Aaronid spokesmen had the true law of Moses without the heresies that contaminated his teachings in the north country. Besides, JE did not take his work seriously.

In response to JE, one of the priests wrote a new torah to reassert the Aaronid claim of exclusive right as Yahweh's spokesmen, and to restore dignity to the holy scriptures. It may well have been the blueprint for Hezekiah's reforms (2 Kings 18:2-8; 2 Chron. 29-31). This unknown author's writings are called the priestly code, the P document, or simply P. If JE is removed from Genesis, Exodus, and Numbers, most of the remainder is P, and virtually all of Leviticus is P. The priestly code was a complete torah in itself, parallel to JE.

P's writings are dignified, terse, legalistic. He frequently used the name Elohim, probably for its prestige. He stressed that the sabbath must be commemorated as a holy day. He provided factual material such as population counts, genealogies, ages, longevities, and place names. He elevated Aaron at Moses' expense, and promoted Solomon's temple as the one central place of worship.

Genesis

Creation. P opened his torah with a majestic account of the creation of the universe, based on the most up to date knowledge of the time. Everything was a chaos of water until the spirit of Elohim brought order. He created light the first day. He created the sky to partition the upper waters from the waters below on the second day. He separated land from water and brought forth vegetation the third day. He created lights in the heavens the fourth day, sea animals and birds the fifth, and land animals and man the sixth. On the seventh day he rested. He blessed and sanctified that day (Gen. 1:1-2:3).

What inspired this wonderful creation story was its reenactment year after year in nature. For when winter snows melted in Armenia and Kurdistan, a torrent rampaged down the Euphrates, overflowing the river banks, spreading across farmlands, raging through city streets and homes. The whole world was an angry, swirling, muddy chaos, and a terrible blackness at night. After many days of flood, the waters gathered into the sea, and dry land reappeared. The rich earth brought forth grass and herbs; trees became laden with fruit. Birds and animals multiplied. People had experienced this awesome event for thousands of years in Sumer and far up the valley. It inspired the Babylonian creation myth, *Enuma Elish*, in which Marduk killed the serpentine, all-engulfing chaos-monster Tiamat and split her carcass to create earth and sky. The story was likely in the Canaanite archives of Jerusalem. P recast it in his own mythological framework in which Elohim was unimaginable, the creator of the world, and ruler of all other gods. Yet P reminds us with a bit of an ancient hymn that "Elohim created man in his own image/ In the image of Elohim created he him/ Male and female created he them" (Gen 1:26-27). Elohim forbids killing for the same reason (Exod. 9:6).

The great flood. P had his own Noah's ark story. It has been fragmented, but it is all there (Gen. 6:9-22; 7:6, 8-9, 11, 13-16, 21, 24; 8:1-2a, 3b-5, 7, 13a, 14-19; 9:1-17). The pieces are intertwined with J's version, but one can easily separate them into two complete stories and lay them out side by side for comparison.

P's version presents a sophisticated view of Elohim; he is distant, majestic, inconceivable; J's Yahweh is man-like, even to his emotions. P dwells on the covenant, with the rainbow as a sign (Gen. 9:1*ff*). In J, Noah's offerings cause Yahweh to regret his actions; he promises never to curse the earth or smite mankind again and offers the seasons for a sign (Gen. 8:20-22). P's flood lasts more than a year, and his Noah sends a raven; J's flood lasts forty days, and his Noah releases a dove. The story came from Sumer, where the god Ea whispered into Ut-Napishtim's reed hut that the other gods were sending a flood to destroy humanity.

Genealogies. Genealogies were useful in deciding privilege and establishing chronology. P probably consulted a book of generations like the Sumerian lists of kings who had amazingly long lives (see below). Examples are in Gen. 6:9-10 and 10:1b-7.

Another Hagar story. After Abram was in the land of Canaan ten years, Sarai, Abram's wife, gave Hagar, her Egyptian maid, to her husband Abram to be his *wife*. Hagar bore Abram a son, and *Abram*, not a god, named him Ishmael. Abram was eighty-six years old when Hagar bore Ishmael to Abram (Gen. 6:3, 15-16). That's it! P omitted frills.

Covenant with Abraham, Isaac, and Jacob. For P, the circumcision rite was necessary but not sufficient for the covenant with Abraham. Slaves and all those born in his house were to be circumcised. The covenant embraced Isaac, therefore Israel, but not Ishmael or his descendents the Arabs, though circumcision was required (Gen. 17). The covenant included Jacob (Israel), who talked to Elohim and erected, anointed, and offered drink to a stone pillar at Beth-El (Gen. 35:9-15). P believed that Jacob (Israel) and Esau (Edom) married their cousins, not Canaanites (Gen. 27:46-28:9).

Other large sections from the P torah include Abraham's establishing a burial site at Hebron (Gen. 23), genealogies of Edom (Gen. 36), and lists of Jacob's sons and their families who went to Egypt (Gen. 46:6-27). And many small sections and verses from P are intertwined with JE.

Exodus

Theophany. Elohim told Moses, I am Yahweh, and I appeared to Abraham, Isaac, and Jacob, not by my name Yahweh, but as El Shaddai. The latter is translated God Almighty, but the meaning is unknown. Yahweh promised to bring the Israelites to Canaan (Exod. 6:2-12). P listed descendents of Reuben, Simeon, and Levi, including Aaron and Moses. Aaron preceded Moses (Exod. 6:14-25).

Aaron. P stressed that Moses was a poor speaker; Aaron would speak for Moses; besides, he knew magic (Exod. 7:1-13). Thus P proved the Aaronid claim of authority over the Mosaic priests.

The plagues. P listed five plagues, including the first, second, and tenth. The third (mosquitoes) and sixth (boils) were unique to P.

Passover. P itemized the passover ceremony, with lamb and unleavened bread (Exod. 12:1-20). He required circumcision for non-Israelites living among them who kept the passover (Exod. 40-49).

Crossing the Red Sea. Yahweh led the Israelites by day in a pillar of cloud and by night in a pillar of fire. He told Moses to lure Pharaoh across the sea. When Pharaoh was near,

Yahweh told Moses to lift his rod and extend his hand to divide the sea so that the Israelites could go on dry ground. After the Israelites crossed, and when the Egyptians were in the midst of the sea, Yahweh told Moses to stretch his hand to drown the army. And the waters covered them (Exod. 13:21-22; 14:1-4, 8-9a, 10a, 10c, 15-18, 21a, 21c, 22-23, 26-29). Aaron was not involved; he was added to the Moses stories late. P made him Moses' brother (Exod. 6:20; 7:1).

The covenant. The same day the Israelites left Egypt, they came to Sinai (Exod. 19:1), and Elohim spoke from the mount to those encamped below, I am Yahweh your god, etc., and announced ten commandments, stressing that the sabbath was holy because Yahweh rested, blessed, and hallowed that day (Exod. 20:1-17). [Dtr[1] used P's list, but added that the sabbath is also holy because Yahweh led them out of Egypt (Deut. 5:15). P and D knew what was written on the tablets in the ark in their own times.] A cloud covered the mount six days, and the glory of Yahweh stood there like fire, and the seventh day he called Moses from the cloud. P said nothing about golden calves or breaking tablets.

So then, and not until then, Moses went up the mount (Exod. 24:15b-18a) to receive long instructions about offerings, ark, tabernacle, furnishings (Exod. 25-27). Thus P intended to settle disputations about temple furnishings and ritual in Hezekiah's reign. Aaron and his descendents would be high priest (Exod. 28:1); Moses and his descendents were assistants. Rest on the sabbath was a perpetual covenant, for Yahweh had rested on the sabbath. Violators would be executed (Exod. 31:12-17).

Yahweh gave Moses two tablets of stone written with the finger of Elohim (Exod. 31:18), and Moses brought them down (Exod. 34:29). Moses' face was hideous from exposure to the glory of Yahweh, so he hid it. The people recited the covenant and repeated the sabbath commandment with the death penalty. They made offerings and carried out the other instructions (Exod. 34:29-40:38), including placing the commandments in the ark (Exod. 40:20). The ark would rest between two huge winged animals in the tabernacle that would be placed in the holy of holies in Solomon's temple. Contradicting JE's permitting numerous shrines, P proved that Moses allowed only one place (Solomon's temple) for worship, and he repeated that through Leviticus and Numbers.

Leviticus

P was responsible for the entire book of Leviticus, except for two short sections that a later editor wrote. Leviticus is a continuation of regulations, instructions, and laws that Yahweh gave Moses after the tabernacle was built and furnished, and the priests outfitted and instructed in their duties.

There are ancient dietary laws (Lev. 11), and ritual purity laws (Lev. 13-15). There was a ritual of sacrificing one goat to Yahweh and releasing another into the wilderness for Azazel. Most translations substitute "scapegoat" for the Hebrew word, "Azazel." Apparently Azazel was the god of a desert tribe who had to give him up when they adopted Yahweh. Yahwists considered him an evil god who still lived out in the desert (Lev. 16). After the exile his goat was loaded with guilt in a ritual of atonement.

P incorporated a holiness code of the Aaronid priests that ends with favors and curses as in a treaty (Lev. 17-26). Within the code is a section from the nomadic era (Lev. 18). Child sacrifice is forbidden (Lev. 18:21). It includes ten commandments: be holy; respect your parents; keep the sabbath; make no idols or gods; about peace offerings; leave food unharvested for strangers; no stealing; no lying; no profane use of Elohim's name; no cheating (Lev. 19:1-13). This set appears to be an early version of the usual set (Exod. 20; Deut. 5) but not as primitive as J's (Exod. 34).

Numbers

P's contribution to Numbers begins with a census of the twelve legendary tribes as they started for the land of Canaan (Num. 1:1-9:14; 10:1-12; 10:14-27; 13:1-16). Their complaints angered Yahweh, who condemned them to wander in the desert forty years and die there. Joshua, chief of the tribe of Ephraim, and Caleb, leader of Judah, would be the only ones to enter Canaan (Num. 14:26-39). More laws and illustrations of piety and obedience follow. A man was stoned for gathering sticks on the sabbath. On Mount Hor, Aaron gave his priestly garments to his son, then died (Num. 20:22-29). The Israelites were to drive out the Canaanites and destroy shrines and idols (Num. 33:50-56). The Levites claimed forty-eight cities and surrounding land (Num. 35:1-8). Moses was given many, many instructions.

JE's contribution to Numbers ended at Num. 25:5; everything after that came from P's torah but for an editor's additions (Num. 28, 29, 33:1-49, and small sections).

Now the Aaronid priests had a torah at least as good as JE's that proved that Yahweh intended the Aaronid priests to rule Solomon's temple, and the Mosaic priests to help them. It contained Leviticus in addition to parts of Genesis, Exodus, and Numbers. It probably occupied two to three scrolls. It included the grand creation story, the flood, patriarchs, Moses stories, laws including two sets of ten commandments, rituals and trappings of Solomon's temple, and Aaron's and Moses' deaths. The P torah may have provided guidance for Hezekiah's reform.

Another century rolled by. Hezekiah died, and his son Manasseh took the throne. Assyria forced him to swear fealty and pay tribute. Out of fright, Manasseh called on every superstition for protection. He put the shrines back up to all the gods. He sacrificed his son and killed many other innocent people. Scythian invasions drew the Assyrian armies away, but Amon maintained his father's superstitions. His servants murdered him after two years, and Josiah ruled under the guidance of a regency. When Josiah was of age, Hilkiah found the D document, a hitherto unknown speech of Moses. It concentrated on worship in Solomon's temple alone, expulsion of other cults, and prohibition of child sacrifice and fertility cults. Dtr[1] quickly expanded D into virtually the present book of Deuteronomy, providing three speeches in which Moses said some things he had not been able to say before. Deuteronomy provided a fitting culmination for the priestly code as well as for JE's torah. Dtr[1] soon followed Deuteronomy with the books of Joshua, Judges, Samuel, and Kings. The reign of Josiah, the ideal king, formed the ending and climax for Kings and the entire series of books: "...And like unto him was there no king before him, that turned to Yahweh with all his heart, and with all his soul, and with all his might, according to the law of Moses."

6

Exile

Nahum crowed over the imminent destruction of Ninevah as Babylonia invaded Assyria's homeland in 612 BC (Nahum 1-3). Babylonia's armies swept through Syria in 609, and Pharaoh Necho rushed up the coast to aid Assyria's remaining forces. Eager for Assyria's end, King Josiah foolishly tried to cut Necho off at Megiddo, and Necho killed him.

The Israelites acclaimed Josiah's brother Jehoahaz as their king. He refused to listen to Jeremiah's advice; hadn't it gotten Josiah killed? But Necho, now master of Syria and Palestine, removed Jehoahaz and installed Jehoahaz' brother, Eliakim. Necho renamed Eliakim as Jehoiakim to show his vassalage and required him to pay tribute. But Necho promised to protect him from Babylonia.

Jeremiah and his friend Urijah advised Jehoiakim to maintain Josiah's reforms, be loyal to Yahweh, and seek an alliance with Babylonia against Egypt. But Jehoiakim pointed out that Josiah's loyalty to Yahweh had not protected him in the prime of life, and that Egypt's armies were at the ready.

Jeremiah replied that Yahweh's memory was long; Yahweh had killed Josiah for Manasseh's sins, so Jehoiakim should do everything he could to please Yahweh. Besides, he argued, Babylonia was a reviving giant that would defeat Egypt. But it was not at all clear to Jehoiakim and his family what the safest course was, so he put the altars up again to please all the gods, and he sent tribute to Necho.

Jeremiah and Urijah made their fears public, so the king and his family condemned them to death for disloyalty. Urijah fled to Egypt, to be brought back and executed. Jeremiah argued that Hezekiah did not kill Micah for warning of the Assyrian danger, but asked him to enlist Yahweh's help. Jeremiah's old friend, Ahikam the son of Shaphan, defended him, and he was acquitted provided he stayed out of the temple (Jer. 26).

In 606 BC Nebupolassar of Babylonia gave Assyria the final blow at Carchemish in Syria. Necho rushed his army to Carchemish, but Nebupolassar's son, Nebuchadrezzar, defeated Necho and took over Syria. Nebuchadrezzar became king of Babylonia in 604 BC.

The Babylonian Menace

Jeremiah thought that Yahweh was sending Babylonia to punish Judah for her sins. He saw ample reason for punishment, for the royalty, priests, and public had gone back to their old ways. Jeremiah had to let everyone know what Yahweh had been telling him, so he dictated all of his revelations from the beginning of his career. Baruch wrote them down, then read Jeremiah's testimony to the crowds in the temple on a holy day.

Micaiah, a grandson of Shaphan, heard Baruch's reading, and told the king's advisors in the scribe's room of the palace. They sent for Baruch and had him read the scroll. They became alarmed and decided to tell the king. They sent Baruch and Jeremiah into hiding, then let the king know of his testimony.

As Jehoiakim listened to the reading of the scroll, he cut off each section as soon as it was read, and threw it into the fire. Once the scroll was burnt up, he ordered the arrest of Baruch and Jeremiah, but they were gone (Jer. 36).

Jeremiah and Baruch rewrote the scroll in their place of refuge. It survives in the book of Jeremiah; Jer. 25 is the introduction, and Jer. 1-18 the body.

Invasion of the Coastal Plain

Nebuchadrezzar led his armies down the coastal plain. Jeremiah came out of hiding and advised sending him tribute. Jehoiakim did so for three years, then rebelled. Occupied elsewhere, Nebuchadrezzar sent armed bands of Chaldeans, Aramaeans, Moabites, and Ammonites to raid throughout Judah, thus disrupting and weakening the nation (2 Kings 24:2). Jeremiah faulted Jehoiakim for "shedding much innocent blood." Judeans fled the country or came into the walls of Jerusalem. Even nomads such as the Rechabites took shelter. Jeremiah praised the Rechabites' faithfulness to their patriarch as a model of obedience (Jer. 35). Habakkuk wrote a prayer for Yahweh's help between 604 and 597 BC (Hab. 1-3). His psalm has musical instructions, showing that it was used in public supplications for Yahweh's mercy (Hab. 3).

Babylonia's First Invasion of Judah

In 598 Jehoiakim died, and his son Jehoiachin was king. But Jehoiachin refused to pay tribute, so Nebuchadrezzar besieged Jerusalem in 597. Egypt did not help Judah as promised. After three months of siege, Jehoiachin and his family came out to surrender. Nebuchadrezzar took them into captivity along with ten thousand of their countrymen: priests, laborers, craftsmen, smiths. He wanted to weaken Judah's capacity to rebel, and at the same time rebuild war-weary Babylonia. Nebuchadrezzar plundered the temple. He made Zedekiah, a son of Josiah, king of Judah. Jeremiah stayed in Jerusalem and advised Zedekiah to obey Yahweh and Nebuchadrezzar (Jer. 20-24, 27).

Four years later, Nebuchadrezzar called Zedekiah to Babylon to renew his oath of fealty. Hananiah, Ahab, and Seraiah the lord chamberlain went with the king. Jeremiah gave Seraiah a magical curse against Babylon to recite and throw into the Euphrates River when he got to Babylon (Jer. 51:59-64).

In Babylon, Hananiah thought he saw signs of collapse and told the captives that Jeremiah shared his hopes (Jer. 29:31). After returning to Jerusalem, Hananiah announced that Yahweh had broken Nebuchadrezzar's power and would return the captives and temple treasures in two years (Jer. 28).

Jeremiah was not so confident that his magical curse was taking effect so soon. He replied, "Amen, may Yahweh do it! but prophets have been wrong before. We will know when it happens." He wrote the captives to ignore such rumors and not expect release soon; i.e., don't revolt. It could take seventy years—*you* may not see freedom, *but you are enjoying life*! So relax and exploit Babylonia's bounties. Build homes, marry, have children, build up your numbers, and pray Yahweh for deliverance. Yahweh plans to bring the Israelites back to Jerusalem and a future of peace in his good time. So be patient and wait. But I warn you that here in Jerusalem, Yahweh is getting angry at the people, your brothers, and Zedekiah, for disobedience (Jer. 29).

Also in Jerusalem, Joel lamented the Babylonian invasion but admitted that it was a well-deserved punishment for disobedience to Yahweh. Now that Judah has learned a lesson, Yahweh will destroy Babylonia in a great and terrible day. An everlasting age of peace and prosperity will follow (Joel 1:1-2-27).

In Babylonia, Ezekiel, an angry spokesman for Yahweh, began to speak to the exiles. He was kept informed about events in Jerusalem, for by the sixth year he raged that the priests in

Solomon's temple worshipped Babylonian gods (Ezek. 8), and that the people celebrated the death and resurrection of the agricultural god Tammuz (Ezek. 8:14). Ezekiel wrote extensively about the coming destruction of Jerusalem (Ezek. 9-23). From his exhortations we discover that it was customary to sacrifice children in Judah (Ezek. 20:37-39). Indeed, *Yahweh had required it*: "...I gave them statutes that were not good... and I polluted them in their own gifts, in that they caused to pass through the fire all that openeth the womb, that I might make them desolate, to the end that they might know that I am Yahweh" (Ezek. 20:25-26). By the ninth year Ekeziel expected the destruction of the temple (Ezek. 24).

Babylonia's Second Invasion of Judah

Nebuchadrezzar's subjects revolted throughout Palestine and Syria. Zedekiah rebelled in 587, so Nebuchadrezzar besieged Jerusalem in 586. Zedekiah jailed Jeremiah (Jer. 32-34). After eighteen months of siege, Nebuchadrezzar caught Zedekiah trying to escape with his army. Zedekiah was punished too horribly to describe here. A month later Nebuchadrezzar's army arrived to destroy Jerusalem and its walls. They took a second group of exiles. The ark of the covenant was no more (Jer. 3:16), for the temple was burnt and razed.

The book of Lamentations describes the awful slaughter and destruction. An unknown man whose family had been massacred wrote it shortly afterward in Palestine. He expected Egypt to intervene, and he praised Zedekiah (Lam. 4:17, 20). His trust in Egypt and praise for Zedekiah prove that the author of Lamentations was not Jeremiah, despite tradition.

After these newest captives reached Babylonia, Ezekiel described the widespread devastation and angrily denounced Edom, Moab, and Ammon for ganging up with Babylonia against Judah (Ezek. 33:21ff, 25). Ezekiel gleefully looked for

Babylonia to destroy them. He waxed poetic for years on the coming destruction of Tyre and Egypt (Ezek. 26-32). Nebuchadrezzar did consolidate his gains in Palestine and began a determined siege of Tyre. But Egypt supplied Tyre by sea, and after thirteen years of siege, Nebuchadrezzar won only a compromise, and withdrew without piercing her walls.

Babylonia's Third Invasion of Judah

Judah, massively depopulated and devastated after years of war, was now destitute and forlorn. Gone were the leaders and workers. Infants, the aged, the crippled, the helpless remained. But they did not expect the exiles back, and so they had their pick of abandoned homes and farms. They were the survivors of the Babylonian war and the owners of the land. Nebuchadrezzar appointed Gedaliah, Shaphan's grandson, as governor of Judah. He gave the squatters legal ownership to encourage restoration.

The prince Ishmael and his friends regarded Gedaliah as a traitor and killed him in 582 BC. Babylonia put down Ishmael's rebellion and took a third group into exile.

A contingent of Israelite soldiers fled to Egypt, taking Jeremiah with them. The soldiers may have been the group that established a colony at Elephantine in the south of Egypt. Dtr^2, presumably Jeremiah, updated the book of Kings, "Neither after Josiah did any like him arise. Yet Yahweh did not turn from his wrath against Judah, on account of Manasseh's provocations..." (2 Kings 23:25c-27, etc.). He made many additions to Deuteronomy that described exile and forced worship of idols (i.e., Deut. 4:25-31). One addition looked toward the exiles' return to Judah (Deut. 30:1-10). Jeremiah, or a disciple, went on lamenting and looking to the future (Jer. 31). He predicted that Babylonia would invade Egypt, which she did in 568 BC, though unsuccessfully. He hoped that Israel and Judah would return, and that Yahweh would make a *new covenant* with them.

Some refugees gradually came back to Judah, and settlers from neighboring countries moved in, but the land remained underpopulated for years.

The Exiles in Babylonia

Babylonia needed the captives to replace soldiers gone to war, to rebuild her cities and plant idle farmlands. She put the Israelites to work at construction, farming, and irrigation projects. She wanted them to settle in and merge with her own people.

By the rivers of Babylon, the exiles wept to think of Zion (Ps. 137). They mourned the holy city: "They have laid Jerusalem on heaps... there was none to bury them" (Ps. 79). They grieved the loss of Solomon's temple: "They have cast fire into the sanctuary" (Ps. 74).

But many adopted Babylonian customs. The great cities were exciting centers of literature, astrology, mathematics, and primitive sciences. The Israelites adopted Babylonian names for themselves, and for the months—even Tammuz!

Ezekiel

The exiles were angry that Yahweh had punished them. The Zadokite priest Ezekiel directed their anger at those who had disobeyed Yahweh, for he had punished Israel for breaking the covenant with him (Ps. 106). Ezekiel was the great spiritual leader of the exiles' search for understanding the holocaust and for learning what Yahweh wanted of them.

If Ezekiel spoke the way he wrote, he must have been a powerful speaker. The young priests in exile listened to him and gradually transformed Yahwism into Judaism. The

Zadokite priests, descendents of Aaron, took the leadership in scholarship in their efforts to learn Yahweh's will.

Ezekiel's visions have captured the imaginations of readers ever since. In 592, the fifth year of exile, he saw Yahweh seated on his chariot-throne above the sapphire sky, in the style of the emperors and the Assyrian sun god (Ezek. 1:4-28, 3:10-15). Probably Ezekiel knew the prophetic traditions of Elijah, Samuel, and Isaiah. But he disclaimed divinity: he was only a "son of man," a mere mortal. Centuries later that term would take on a supernatural meaning.

Psalmists wailed, "O Elohim, why have you cast us off for ever?" for their fathers' sins (Ps. 74). Ezekiel replied, "Yahweh will not punish anyone for his ancestors' sins. He is merciful and just. He will forgive any sinner who repents and turns to righteousness" (Ezek. 18). And gradually the exiles came to believe that Yahweh was not only in Jerusalem but with them in Babylonia.

As time went on, ageing men, impatient to return home, asked, "Can these dry bones live? Our bones are dry; our hope is gone." What could Ezekiel say as long as Babylon held them captive? He replied that Yahweh would open the graves to take them back to Jerusalem (Ezek. 37). Out of despair and futility was born a promise of resurrection.

Ezekiel and his followers hoped to build a new Jerusalem and temple after their return (Ezek. 37). They also hoped that the exiles from the northern kingdom, Israel, would return, and that Judah and Israel would again be one kingdom, the house of Israel. Jehoiachin and his sons would be princes, so the house of David would continue under Yahweh the king. Yahweh would make a covenant of peace (Ezek. 34:24; 45:7). In 573 Ezekiel presented a plan for the future temple and city (Ezek. 40ff). Nebuchadrezzar gave up his siege of Tyre in 572 and failed to conquer Egypt in 568 BC, despite Ezekiel's eager anticipation of their destruction   (Ezek. 26-32). There is reason to believe that much of the book of Ezekiel was written by his disciples.

Each city had temples to Marduk and other Babylonian gods, and the masters expected the exiles to participate in the national cults so that the gods would keep smiling on the empire. Ezekiel taught the exiles not to accept the gods of their captors. Israelite priests insisted that Israelites must worship only Yahweh: "I will lift up mine eyes unto the hills, from whence cometh my help..." (Ps. 121). But loyalty was difficult amidst those temples of such awesome size and beauty, especially for children who married Babylonian playmates who would naturally place trust in their own gods.

Separateness was key to survival of the exiles as Israelites. They knew well that their cousins of the northern kingdom had blended with the captor populations. More than ever before, the priests insisted on marriage with their own kind, on the sanctity of the sabbath, and on distinctive features such as fringes, phylacteries, skullcaps, headbands, and sharp corners on the beard.

Revision of the Prophets

The exiles searched the writings of Amos, Hosea, Isaiah I, and Micah for prophetic words that would feed hope. Such prophecies were hard to find, so revisionists inserted them into those books. Examples are the warnings of the destruction of Judah, already accomplished, and the hope that the Davidic kingdom would be restored; these words were put into Amos' mouth (Amos 2:4-5; 9:11-15). Other additions include Amos 1:9-12 and 9:8b-10.

These additions should be read in terms of Dtr[1]'s past hope that Josiah's reign would be a long one, and that his descendents would continue his reforms. Jehoiachin and his descendents were still alive and hearing Ezekiel's and other priests' teachings about Yahweh's will. And naturally their friends, whether in exile or not, would like to see the royal family, David's descendents, resume their rule as kings of an independent Israel-Judah.

Visions of the New Israel

Nebuchadrezzar died in 561 BC. His son, Amel-Marduk, pardoned Jehoiachin and released him from prison (2 Kings 25:27-30). Amel-Marduk was murdered the next year, and in the ensuing turmoil, Babylonia's strength declined. Hope of a general release of the captives was countered by fear that nomadic horsemen of central Asia, the Scythians or Cimmerians, could maraud and slaughter the settled peoples of the Fertile Crescent without opposition from Babylonia. Ezekiel admitted that "Gog of Magog" may attack Judah after the return. The mythical King Gog symbolized the wild horsemen. "Magog," properly meaning, "the land of Gog," was misinterpreted as a second mythical lawless man. So now there were two mythical lawless men, Gog and Magog. The developing myth would become all-important in later centuries. Ezekiel merely argued that that fears of nomadic raiders was blown out of proportion; if Israel is faithful to Yahweh, he will destroy all invaders, and eventually Israel will flourish in peace (Ezek. 38-39).

Cyrus of Persia took over Media in 550 BC and Sardis of Asia Minor in 546. His empire would stabilize the Middle East. A sage among the exiles, known to us only as Second Isaiah, looked for Cyrus to liberate the captive Israelites from Babylonia, and protect Israel from other invaders (Is. 40-35). Cyrus was the anointed one of Yahweh, a messiah (Is. 44:21-45:7). When they were slaves in Egypt, Yahweh chose the Israelites for a model of righteousness for the nations. They had failed in his eyes, so he had sent them back into slavery.

They had repented, so Yahweh offered them a new covenant. Now the Jews, full of hope, were about to make a second exodus to a New Israel and a New Jerusalem. The New Israel would be a model of righteousness for the nations; the whole world would see the light and join in worshipping Yahweh and obeying his laws (Is. 45:13*ff*, 49:22*ff*). Second Isaiah wrote four songs about Israel the loving servant of Yahweh (Is. 42, 49, 50) who had been punished for the people's sins and who will be restored (Is. 52:13-53:12). Still more was added later to the book of Isaiah in expectation of the return (Is. 60-62), including a psalm (Is. 63:7-64:11).

7

The New Israel

The Jews Return

The people of Babylon welcomed Cyrus the Great into their city as their liberator in 539 BC. The next year he issued an edict freeing the captives. He appointed Shesh-Bazzar high commissioner of Judah to rebuild Jerusalem and the temple (Ezra 1). Cyrus granted these liberties to cut the stress on his far-flung armies. The Jews—the captives were no longer Israelites, but Jews—were exuberant. Their poets wrote lavish praises of Cyrus, Israel's saviour, the anointed one of Yahweh (Is. 44:21-45:7). The "seventy years" of exile that Jeremiah mentioned turned out to be nearly that—fifty-nine—two generations, or a full life-time. Few of the original captives were still alive. Shesh-Bazzar, prince of Judah, who was probably Shenazar son of King Jehoiachin (1 Chron. 3:18), led a group to Judah at once. Others filtered back over the centuries. Many stayed in Babylonia, which was to outlast Jerusalem as a great center of Judaic learning.

Shesh-Bazzar rebuilt the altar in the ruins of Solomon's temple and resumed sacrificial offerings to gain Yahweh's protection from the "people of the land," for the residents thought the land was theirs; their parents and grandparents had taken over vacant properties and rebuilt the tumble-down homes. The residents included Ammonites, Edomites, bedouins, Ashdodites, and other aliens whose forefathers may have plundered and burnt Jerusalem. Some residents were Israelites never taken into captivity, while others were Samaritans; both still followed the primitive Yahwism of pre-exilic days.

The Jews—the returnees—claimed to be the remnant of Yahweh's chosen people. They had acquired much learning and sophistication in the great civilization of Babylonia. They had suffered the brunt of Yahweh's wrath for the sins of all the people, so they had special understanding, duties, and privileges. They had undertaken an exhaustive soul-searching to discover Yahweh's will, so they had insights that no one else could have. And they could prove that they were the rightful heirs of their forefathers' properties. For all these reasons, Jews and residents hated and fought each other. Obadiah angrily proclaimed that the Jews would destroy the foreigners in a great day of Yahweh and reconquer all of Canaan. Thus Yahweh would once again be sovereign in the land (Obad. 1:1-21).

The Second Temple

The Jews began to rebuild the temple the second year (Ezra 3). Shesh-Bazzar refused to let the "people of the land" be employed in this public works project. In retaliation, the residents interfered with reconstruction (Ezra 4:1-5). They told the Persian overlords that the Jews were rebuilding without permission and that they planned to revolt once the wall was restored. On top of all this, the returnees had to grub out their own meager living, and so rebuilding languished.

Haggai

Time passed. Zerubbabel, nephew of Shesh-Bazzar and a descendant of David, became governor. When Darius I became king of Persia in 522 BC, Haggai urged Zerubbabel and the people to finish the temple, for that was Yahweh's will (Hag.

1:1-15) The Jews requested Darius' authorization to rebuild, insisting that Cyrus' edict must be in his archives. Darius had a search made. Cyrus' edict was found, and Darius ordered rebuilding to proceed.

Haggai may have seen Solomon's temple before it was destroyed in 586; in 522, he was an old man remembering its awesome size and beauty. But the glory of the second temple would be greater than that of the first. The nations would submit to Yahweh, so Israel would have peace (Hag. 1:6-9, 20-23). Unclean people—those who were not Jews—were not to be employed in the rebuilding of the temple (Hag. 2:11-18).

Zechariah

Zechariah said that Yahweh had forgiven the Jews for the sins for which he had punished them. He exulted that Zerubbabel would continue the Davidic dynasty as king, and that Joshua would be high priest in the tradition of Ezekiel. Those two anointed ones would rule in harmony (Zech. 3:1-8; 4:14). But Zechariah's hopes did not entirely come true, he did not mention Zerubbabel in a restatement (Zech. 6:12-13), and he assured the reader that Joshua was the true branch of David. Zechariah hoped that Yahweh would again live in the temple and protect his people and that Jerusalem would again be a great city (Zech. 8).

David's descendents never ruled again, although some were still around in the Greek period (Zech. 12:12; Zech. 9-14 was added after Alexander destroyed the Persian empire). The Aaronid priests ruled Israel until the Maccabean revolt.

A disciple of Second Isaiah celebrated the joyful completion of the temple in 515 BC (Is. 60:1-4*ff*) .

Persian Dualism

Existence of evil in the world has been explained many ways at different times. Around the time of the Jewish return from exile, the prophet Zoroaster of Persia taught that God had created a good spirit called Mazda-Ahura, Ormazd, or Mithra, symbolized by fire, light, the sun. That spirit of purity created all good things. He created human beings with immortal souls.

God also created Ahriman, a spirit who rebelled, and who created every kind of evil, including venomous snakes, toxic plants, and vicious beasts. Good and evil have become intermixed in the universe, hence strife is everywhere. Ultimately Mazda and his followers will win and banish Ahriman into outer darkness forever.

The Jews probably received full exposure to dualism during the Persian era. Judaism officially rejected it, for God created all, whether good or evil, light or darkness (Is. 45:7). But Satan, God's antagonist, appears as a definite personality in Zech. 3. And the ancient story in Genesis of the snake who led innocent humanity into temptation would now be read in terms of dualism.

Job

The book of Job is an adaptation of an ancient Babylonian story intended to probe the nature and existence of God. The preface and ending are still in Babylonian style. It has echoes of the Marduk-Tiamat myth, with Yahweh master of monsters (Job 40:15; 41:1; also note Is. 27:31, Ps. 74:13-14). It was probably written by a Jew in Palestine at the time of increasing influence of Aramaic on Hebrew (about 500 BC). Job was a famous sage or mythical figure (Ezek. 14:14, 20). Satan was not Yahweh's enemy but his servant, and humanity's enemy and supervisor. His wager with Yahweh reveals how tongue-in-cheek the story was. The book ridiculed the covenant and the Deuteronomist's claim that evil befalls those unfaithful to God. An editor added Elihu's pious claim that one must not question Yahweh but continue praising him even in adversity (Job 36:24) and keep faith even when knowledge and understanding fail (Job 32-37).

Malachi

The author of this book calls himself Malachi. It means "my messenger." He makes it clear that priests were Yahweh's messengers (Mal. 2:7). Malachi may have been a pen name rather than a personal name. He lamented that the people were stingy in tithing, and their offerings were blemished. The priests did not follow Yahweh's laws. And Jews were even marrying Gentiles.

Malachi or other priests in Jerusalem had complained to the Jewish community in Babylonia or Persia about the shortcomings in Jerusalem, the model of righteousness for the nations. So that community was sending a messenger to straighten everything out in Jerusalem (Mal. 3:1). Now, remember that a priest is Yahweh's messenger. The messenger who was coming to Jerusalem was probably Ezra.

Ezra, Priest and Scribe of the Law of Moses

Xerxes I became king of Persia in 486 BC. He captured Athens but his tide was reversed at Salamis six years later. Throughout his reign and that of Artaxerxes I (464-423), the Jews' enemies fought the reconstruction of Jerusalem and its walls.

In 458 BC, Ezra, an Aaronid priest, arrived in Jerusalem armed with the "law of Moses" and Artaxerxes' authority to impose it upon Judah (Ezra 7). A large group of returnees came with him (Ezra 8). He called a great assembly of the people for Sukkot, and he read from the "book of the law" each of the seven days (Neh. 8). He read instructions for the feast (Neh. 8:14-15), probably from Lev. 23-39-43. Deuteronomy does not give directions for Sukkot (Deut. 16:13-15; 31:10), so it was not the entire book of the law for Ezra. *Ezra's book of the law was probably the Torah, the five books of Moses.* Ezra dissolved the marriages of Jews wed to foreigners (Ezra 9-10), and he held a ceremony of atonement for the sin of mixed marriage (Neh. 9). Ezra cleansed the land for Yahweh in fulfillment of Malachi 3:1. It must have been a pretty tough time for all.

Nehemiah

Nehemiah came from Susa, Persia, in 445 BC to govern and direct the reconstruction of Jerusalem and its walls. The residents (Samaritans led by Sanballat, and Ammonites, Ashdodites, and Arabs) were still harassing the reconstruction. But Nehemiah completed the city wall, and then Jerusalem attracted large numbers of settlers (Neh. 3:33-7:5). He went back to Persia in 433, planning to return to Jerusalem, but there is no record that he ever did.

The Jewish leaders were resolved to create a kingdom ruled by Yahweh as a model for the nations to follow. That was how they could achieve a permanent peace. Having learned the dire consequences of disobedience to Yahweh, they would search the Torah and pray to learn Yahweh's will, and they would teach nothing but that. To be Yahweh's chosen people, an example for the world, was a great burden, hard to bear, and Judaism could be a strict, demanding, harsh religion.

The Final Redactor of the Torah

As we saw, Ezra brought the Pentateuch or Torah to Jerusalem, and it became the law of the land. Since ancient times, many Bible students have thought that he wrote or edited the Torah. Spiritual descendent of Ezekiel, Ezra would have had all the resources of the community of Jewish scholars in Babylonia at his command.

Whoever he was, the final editor of the Torah is called R, the redactor. He wanted to solve the problem of conflicting torahs (JE, D, and P), each with its partisans. The Mosaic priests claimed to be the direct descendents of Moses, but even in exile, and after the return, they took orders from the Aaronid priests. The Aaronid priests claimed to be the only spokesmen for Moses and Yahweh, and they could prove it with the P document. So the old fight between Israel and Judah went on with Yahweh backing both sides. Combining the legal books would at least force them to argue from the same books. The result was the Torah: Genesis, Exodus, Leviticus, Numbers, and Deuteronomy as we have them today.

R used P as the framework for the first four books. He cut it into pieces and fitted corresponding sections of JE into that framework as far as possible. He left out little, since it all came from Moses, and he had to satisfy both camps. He also used other sources such as the book of the generations of Adam. Where needed, he composed short introductions, transitions, explanations, and summaries. Sometimes he wrote longer sections to give the law as he thought it should be. His style is terse, dignified, pedantic, and hard to distinguish from P's. We will look at examples of R's work in each book of the Torah.

Genesis

Creation. The redactor used P's majestic creation story as a dignified introduction to the entire Torah (Gen. 1:1-2:3). R wrote a brief summary: *These are the generations of the heavens and the earth, when they were created* (Gen. 2:4a). He then inserted JE's stories of the creation of man, expulsion, Cain and Abel, and genealogies to Seth (Gen. 2:4b-4:26).

The genealogies. R inserted a section from the book of the generations of Adam (BGA), which lists the descendents of Adam: *This is the book of the generations of Adam...*, and so on to Lamech (Gen. 5:1-28). Then from JE a verse about Noah (Gen. 5:29). Then more from BGA about Lamech and Noah: *And Lamech lived after he begat Noah five hundred ninety-five years, and begat sons and daughters, and all the days of Lamech were seven hundred seventy-seven years, and he died. And Noah was five hundred years old, and Noah begat Shem, Ham, and Japheth* (Gen. 5:30-32).

Noah and the flood. A piece from JE leads into the Noah and flood story (Gen. 6:1-8). But the real stuff begins with P (Gen. 6:9-22, etc., as listed on page 59). The redactor intertwined P's story with JE's, including these passages from BGA: *And Noah was six hundred years old when the flood of waters was upon the earth* (Gen. 7:6). *And Noah lived after the flood three hundred and fifty years, and all the days of Noah were nine hundred and fifty years, and he died. Now these are the generations of the sons of Noah, Shem, Ham, and Japheth* (Gen. 9:28-10:1a).

Exodus

The redactor listed the tribes of Israel in Egypt as an introduction to this book (Exod. 1:1-5). Again he intertwined JE into P's framework: Yahweh's call to Moses, the plagues, the flight. His own compositions are brief, e.g., Elohim speaks, Moses replies (Exod. 3:4b), and Yahweh announces his intention to free the Israelites (Exod. 6:13).

R frequently inserted, *Yahweh hardened Pharaohs heart and would not let the people go* (Exod. 9:35, 10:20, etc.) to show that it was Yahweh's plan, not Pharaoh's.

R probably used a separate list of stations as the source for his brief notes tracing the route of the Israelites, e.g.: *And the children journeyed from Rameses to Succoth...* (Exod. 12:37a) *And they took their journey from Succoth and encamped in Etham, in the edge of the wilderness* (Exod. 13:20).

After JE's song of the sea, R summarized the crossing: *For the horse of Pharaoh went in... but... Israel went on dry land in the midst of the sea* (Exod. 15:19). After JE's song of Miriam, R inserted a transition: *So Moses brought Israel from the Red Sea* (Exod. 15:22).

Ten commandments. In P, the people came to Sinai, and Elohim gave the ten commandments before Moses went up (Exod. 19:1; 20:1-17; 24:15b-18a). R deftly put in a travel note (Exod. 9:2a), then let JE bring Moses up the mount, down, up, and down again (Exod. 19:2b-25) before Moses recited P's ten commandments (Exod. 20:1-17). R inserted P's ten commandments into a sentence from E as follows: *So Moses went down to the people and spoke to them,* [R inserted P's ten commandments here] *and all the people saw the thunderings, and the lightnings...* (Exod. 19:25-20:18).

Leviticus

This book is entirely P except for the redactor's two compositions: first, instructions for Sukkot (Lev. 23:39-43; p. 82), then Yahweh's threats for disobedience, and the repentance and return of the exiles (Lev. 26:39-45).

Numbers

The first ten chapters are P except for R's small insertions (Num. 3:1, 9:15-23, 10:13, 28). Then he wove JE around the P narrative (Num. 10:29-25:5). After that, it is all P except for R's own insertions. The major R composition are Num. 28-29 and the review of the itinerary (Num. 33:1-49). He or JE wrote a piece that cites older writings, "The Wars of Yahweh" and "Spring up O Well" (Num. 21:12-20).

Deuteronomy

The redactor copied P's account of Yahweh's command to Moses to die in Mount Nebo (Num. 27:12-14) and inserted an expansion of it into Deuteronomy (Deut. 32:48-52). And he transferred P's story of Moses' death from the P version of Numbers (Deut. 34:7-9).

The Torah as the Jewish Canon

Thanks to the redactor, the Jews now had one Torah with greater authority than all other writings. Ezra made the Torah the law of the land, and it became the foundation for everyday life of the Jews. The people held it in such high esteem that it became their canon. That is, it was so sacred that rarely would anyone venture to alter it in any way.

Other Writings after the Return

Ruth. Ezra's stricture against mixed marriages inspired this tale that David's great grandmother was a Moabitess!
Second Joel. About 400 BC, a follower of Joel wrote imaginatively and poetically upon Yahweh's punishment of Judah's

evil neighbors, and a new age of peace. Yahweh will rule from Jerusalem, and Judah shall survive forever (Joel 2:28-3:21).

The Chronicler. About 350 BC, a priest rewrote the history of the Jews from the Zadokite viewpoint. Most of it was taken from the Torah, Samuel, and Kings. The book of Chronicles is usually less historical than the corresponding material in Samuel and Kings. His David and Solomon are ideal kings. Hezekiah also rates high, for the Chronicler glorified his reform. The Chronicler said little about a future king of Judah, for Persia could interpret such as traitorous. But he had a clear vision of everlasting peace.

The Chronicler had sources that we know only from his citations: annals of King David (1 Chron. 27:24) and records of seers (1 Chron. 29:29-30, 2 Chron. 9:29-31, 12:15—see 1 Kings 14:29-31). Those sources were not necessarily factual.

Ezra and Nehemiah. The Chronicler told nothing about the Jews in exile but continued his history with these books. Just in time, too, for the reports from Ezra and Nehemiah were already falling apart. The correct sequence of the reports from Ezra is Ezra 7-8, Neh. 8, Ezra 9-10, Neh. 9. Nehemiah's report consisted of Neh. 1-2, 3:33-7:5, 12:27-13:31. The Chronicler also used other documents.

Psalms. Psalm 126 is about the exiles returning to Judah. Other psalms may have been revised as late as 150 BC.

Jonah. A hilarious parable. Yahweh plays tricks on Jonah, a thick-headed Jew who cannot learn the simple lesson that Yahweh wants submission to his will. All of the children must have laughed with delight at the tricks, but they learned that God would love Ninevah's king, people, and animals more than a disobedient Jew, if only they showed the least bit of repentance. Humorless priests of later ages assumed that the book of Jonah was composed in the time of Jeroboam II because of the obscure prophet Jonah (2 Kings 14:25). The author probably lived in the 300's BC. Extinct Ninevah lent itself to the tale because the ancient Assyrian terror was still vivid in Jewish memory.

The Messianic Hope

The ruling class of every nation puts on impressive coronation ceremonies for new kings, and priests invoke the gods. This is to command the people's allegiance and make them believe that the gods had chosen him to be king over every other candidate. After all, kings have to be somehow more powerful than their rivals, and they want everyone to believe that heavenly might is on their side. Many kings claimed to be gods come to earth in human form, and they required their subjects to worship them in temples built for that purpose. Judaism rejected the notion that kings were gods incarnate, although that idea may lurk behind ancient legends of Enoch and Elijah. Still, the Israelites and Jews always liked the idea that Yahweh chose their rulers. Psalms 2, 72, and 110 were coronation hymns that asserted the divine power and wisdom of the king. Samuel's ceremony of anointing Saul, the first king of Israel, symbolized that he was Yahweh's choice. The word *messiah* simply meant "anointing," and so by extension it meant the chosen one.

The messiah was always human, not a god, even if Yahweh had chosen him. Saul the messiah was a man. After Saul was killed, a new story was told: Yahweh had transferred his favor to David and his descendents. Dtr[1]—Jeremiah—cultivated that story. When David's descendents were dethroned and went into exile with their subjects, the exiles' great hope was to return to Judah with the ruling family restored to its throne. Their wishes came true, except that they remained a part of the Persian empire. Then they hoped for freedom, and that the dynasty would reign forever. Somehow that did not happen, but the temple was rebuilt, and Yahweh dwelt in it. Yahweh ruled the people through the priests; Israel would be a holy nation, a nation of priests, and a light to the world. War could not exist because all countries would submit to the will of Yahweh. Israel would enter a messianic age lasting as long as the earth.

But Israel still needed a real king, a descendent of David; perhaps that would happen if Israel was truly following Yahweh's laws. Can all this take place in a world of mortals? The legend grew that Elijah returned from time to time to see whether Israel was ready for the messiah, and at the passover seder the folk poured a fifth cup of wine for Elijah. Elijah was not the son of David, so he would not be king. But if Elijah saw that everyone in Judah was obeying Yahweh, then a descendent of David would appear. There were still some around. But surely the messiah would be more than a man to achieve eternal peace in the midst of the great empires. And so the myth of the supernatural messiah was born.

We have seen many writings in the Old Testament about worldly matters which could feed hopes of supernatural intervention, in those who are looking for such things, and who have little understanding of why the scriptures were written. In the next chapter, we will see more of the myth of the messiah. Ironically, this Jewish myth turned upon the Jews.

8

The World is About to End

Instead of entering a messianic age, Israel kept getting entangled in the schemes of empires. Alexander the Great of Macedonia conquered Greece, Asia Minor, Egypt, and the Persian empire. After he died, four of his generals (the *Diadochi*, Successors) grabbed their shares. Of the four *Diadochi*, the Ptolemies (Egypt) and the Seleucids (Babylonia-Syria) affected Israel. Gradually the Roman empire gobbled up all four Greek empires, and Israel along with them.

THE AGE OF APOCALYPSE

The great age of apocalyptic literature blossomed under the Seleucids and the Romans, about 200 BC to 200 AD. The writer of apocalypse has given up on hope of peace in the world. He reaches beyond the stars to new worlds, and to the infinite. God has to destroy this world if he wants to triumph over his enemies. He will punish the wicked with everlasting torment and reward the obedient with eternal bliss. The best known apocalypses are the Koran, Daniel, and the Revelation to John.

In the ebb and flow of empires, peoples often saw invaders as liberators bringing justice, peace, and prosperity. Reality seldom came up to their hopes, and never for long. Paranoid, power-hungry emperors killed suspected enemies by the thousands without mercy. Night and day, the lives of millions were filled with terror; they could find no peace in the world. Death was the only escape from the horrors of life. Far sweeter would be life with the gods.

Where were the gods? The gods of the moon, sun, and five planets looked down on earthly mortals. Higher were the stars, which were gods or souls of unborn humans or those dead, or all of these. The sky, blue by day, black by night, separated the world from the abode of the gods. These notions developed in the stone age when the earth was flat. They changed little when the earth became round and Plato's geo centric model of the universe became popular among the educated.

Aristarchus taught that the earth was a planet revolving around the sun. The stars were an enormous distance away, suns, perhaps. The apparent daily rising and setting of all heavenly bodies was explained simply by the spinning of the earth on its axis. But there was little place for the gods in Aristarchus' heliocentric universe.

Aristotle considered the evidence for both theories. He argued that if the earth moves, it should leave the moon behind. Constellations should seem to change shape with the seasons due to parallax of the stars. Neither phenomenon was seen; therefore, the best theory was that the earth stood still. The sky was the sphere of the fixed stars and the boundary of the universe.

Boundaries could not limit the human mind. Thales apparently thought the space outside the universe was filled with water. Sky separated waters above from those below, in P's creation story (Gen. 1:2). Others supposed that space was filled with divine fire (Hieraclites of Ephesus) or divine light (John 1:1-5). Whether filled with divine water, fire, or light, the infinity of space was the domain of the cause of it all, the highest god. The bubble-like universe permitted the most enticing of all hopes: there is a being out there who knows what is going on in this would of ours. That was the Neoplatonic theory of Plotinus.

Thinkers in the Middle East combined Persian dualism with Platonic and Neoplatonic theories to produce a family of gnostic religions. God was pure goodness and light, formless, unknowable, unimaginable, changeless. He had not made the universe; the creator was an ambitious lower god acting without God's knowledge. So the universe, all matter, all flesh, and the ruling gods are evil. The only good in the universe is human souls, the sparks of divinity trapped in the universe and imprisoned in human bodies. When bodies die, souls escape and try to go back to God. But gods watching at the gates of the heavens do not let them pass. Only through some type of special knowledge, *gnosis*, can a soul make its way back to God.

Many gnostic religions have arisen with different notions about what sort of *gnosis* is required for salvation. Most held that a saviour would descend from heaven, destroy the universe, and take human souls back to God. The various forms of gnosticism permeated every major cult throughout the hellenistic Middle East. Judaism flirted with gnosticism and gave birth to numerous offspring religions. Ultimately mainstream Judaism rejected gnosticism.

One did not have to be a gnostic to look for an end to an age of evil. That empires came and went was historical fact. Astrologers taught that the precession of the equinoxes determined the ages of history. The sun was entering the constellation of Aries; the age of the lamb could only be the messianic age. Greek mythology taught that the heroic or bronze age was long dead; it was now time for the iron age to end with its warfare and cruelty. Swords would be made into plowshares. The Jews searched for scriptural evidence of the coming age of peace. Many believed that God's covenants with Noah, Abraham, and Moses marked ages. Since the exile, Israel had renewed its covenant and had become a holy nation. The age of peace was at hand.

Some found a prophecy of the end of an age in Ezekiel's warning that if Babylon fell, nothing would prevent the nomads from attacking Israel, unless Israel won Yahweh's favor through obedience. They focussed on Gog and developed an elaborate myth of the savage leader, an emperor who made his own laws. He would wreak unparalleled misery upon the world before Yahweh destroyed all forces of evil and the age of peace began. Who was Gog? Nearly every generation could point to some such wicked man. They identified certain Seleucid and Roman emperors as Gog, each in his turn.

Students found many such "prophecies" in the scriptures. *Your dead will come back to life* (Is. 26:14). This is part of a section about returning from exile in Babylonia and Assyria (Is. 24-27), probably written in the fifth century BC. The "dead" symbolized Jews who had abandoned Yahweh. If they return to him, then the Jews should accept them. Those who do not come back remain dead to the community (Is. 26:18). But some thought that it was Yahweh's promise of eternal life to the faithful.

The heavens will vanish like smoke, the earth wear out is not about the universe. It expresses hope that Yahweh's protection and justice will endure no matter what happens (Is. 51:5).

The mountains may go away and the hills totter... but my covenant of peace will never leave you. Israel has survived disasters of all sorts. Someday there will be no more war (Is. 54:10). It is a reasonable hope, isn't it?

I am going to create new heavens and a new earth. A chosen few will restore Judah better than it was before the exile (Is. 65:17).

For as the new heavens and the new earth I am making will endure before me, so will your race and your name endure (Is. 66:22). The Jews will never be extinguished or assimilated, but will survive as a model for the nations.

Two verses were stuck on to the end of Malachi, among other additions, to exhort faithfulness to Yahweh under threat of punishment: *Behold, I will send you Elijah the prophet before the coming of the great and dreadful day of Yahweh: And he shall turn the heart of the fathers to the children, and the heart of the children to their father, lest I come and smite the earth with a curse* (Mal. 4:5-6). Elijah visits earth from time to time. Whenever invasion was imminent, the Jews always hoped that Yahweh would help them defeat their enemies and that an age of peace would begin. Under the Seleucids, the passage was taken as a prophecy of the end of the world. And so on.

The Greeks

After Alexander routed the Persians at Issus in Asia Minor in 333 BC, a writer whom we know only as Second Zechariah looked for him to go on to destroy the Persian empire. Alexander would soon conquer the coastal cities; Tyre would not escape this time (Zech. 9:1-8). Jerusalem should welcome Alexander as her new king, for he would bring justice and peace (Zech. 9:9-10:12). He would destroy the Persian army in a dramatic final battle, perhaps at Megiddo where other great armies had been destroyed. Faithful Jews should not worry (Zech. 12). Second Zechariah's hope came true: in 332 BC, Alexander occupied Tyre along with Syria, Palestine, and Egypt without disturbing Jerusalem. He conquered the rest of the Persian empire and spread Greek culture everywhere he went. He designed cities like Alexandria, Egypt, on the Greek style, with temples, gymnasia, theaters, broad avenues; citizens of high standing would govern. Conquered peoples accepted hellenism as the highest civilization yet, and the wave of the future. Everywhere they adopted Greek language, gods, art, science. It was an age of peace.

After Alexander's death in 323, the Ptolemaic empire (Egypt) ruled Judah until losing it to the Seleucids. A Palestinian Jew wrote Ecclesiastes between 300 and 200 BC to tell how empty life is. We should live proper lives, enjoy what we can, and face adversity with resignation. There is no future life, but the spirit goes back to God. We cannot understand God. The books of Judith and Tobit were written to promote faith and courage.

The Samaritans

The Samaritans always insisted on more freedom than the Jews allowed, including the right to worship other gods. Their scriptures consisted of the Torah alone; they rejected the Prophets and Writings and ignored the great debates that modernized Judaism. About the time that Alexander died, the Samaritans made a final break with the Jews and built their own temple on Mount Gerizim.

Angry at their independence of thought, Second Zechariah scolded the straying shepherds, the Samaritan priests (Zech.

11). Yahweh would break the bond between Israel (Samaria) and Judah (Zech. ll:14), and destroy those who would not come to Jerusalem for Sukkot (Zech. 14:16-19). After all, God ruled the world from Jerusalem. These diatribes were added to the book of Zechariah.

The Sadducees

The Zadokites, the family of high priests, now called Sadducees, still formed the aristocratic ruling class of Judah. They were conservative and regarded only the written Torah as holy. They treated the lower priests with contempt and regarded their beliefs in resurrection, angelology, and demonology as superstitions. The lower priests worked intimately with the people, so the Sadducees became increasingly isolated. The Sadducees tolerated hellenism in line with their policy of compromising with occupying powers.

The Hasidim, Pious Ones

The lower priests, descendents of the Mosaic priests, still did the menial work of the temple, including teaching, writing, copying, and sacrificing. They called themselves the Hasidim, the Pious Ones. Some were sages, well versed in the scriptures. Others had little education and earned a living elsewhere, occasionally helping in the temple. Close to the people, the Hasidim wrote for them and led them. The Hasidim shared with the masses their poverty and beliefs in resurrection, angelology, and demonology. They believed that there would soon be a day of judgement followed by resurrection of the dead. They were fervently devoted to the Torah and were ready to lay down their lives for it. They were suspicious of foreign influence, and the Sadducees' hellenization gave them another reason to hate them. The Hasidim gave rise to the Pharisees and Essenes (below).

The Septuagint

Alexandria, Egypt, had a rather large Jewish population who became hellenized. Their scholars translated the scriptures to Greek about 250 BC, in the reign of Ptolemy II Philadelphus. Their translation is called the Septuagint. Literature flourished in Alexandria that urged faithfulness to Jewish ideals, such as Baruch, which tells about the exile, the Prayer of Manasseh, the Martyrdom of Isaiah, and the Testaments of the Twelve Patriarchs. In the last, Reuben said that women lured the ruling angels of the universe down to earth and sired a race of giants (Gen. 6:1-4). The Wisdom of Solomon personified and elaborated on wisdom as coming from God, and promised retribution after death. Chapters 1-11 were written in Hebrew; additions were in Greek.

Life Under the Seleucids

The Jews welcomed the Seleucid invasions in hope of escaping Egyptian taxes. Antiochus III gave Judah low taxes and other privileges, and interfered little. At the end of his reign, 187 BC, Jesus Ben Sira wrote Ecclesiasticus in Alexandria. This book offered some worldly wisdom and a search for religious truth. It taught that there was no resurrection.

Seleucus IV left Judah alone until he raided the temple funds for military expenses and payoffs to Rome. About this time, the book of Esther was written by an unknown author in Palestine to teach that the Jews should trust in God even when foreigners hate them for their distinctive customs and separateness.

Antiochus IV Epiphanes (174-164 BC) made up his mind to hellenize Jerusalem and assimilate the Jews into the empire. In 167 he deposed Onias III the high priest and plundered the temple. He placed a statue of Zeus Olympus, in his own likeness, in the temple and required the Jews to worship him. He outlawed circumcision and other Jewish customs. He killed many Jews who refused to obey his orders.

The Jews realized that they were being persecuted for faithfulness to Yahweh! Searching the scriptures turned up a prediction from Ezekiel that seemed to fit: a wild man would wreak devastation before the age of peace. Antiochus IV was Gog.

Daniel

The desecration of the temple inspired the book of Daniel. The original Daniel was a Canaanite folk hero or sage (Ezek. 14:14, 20, 28:3).

The unknown writer—let us now call *him* Daniel—was probably an Hasidic priest. The book is an allegory to hide the meaning in case the rulers found a copy. The setting, in exile and in Darius' court, symbolized Antiochus' reign. Daniel narrated Antiochus' rise and hoped-for fall, and mourned the exile of Onias III, prince of peace. Only God can help, so be steadfast to Jewish traditions. Be calm while God carries out his mysterious plans. "One like the son of man"—not Cyrus this time, but the emperor of Rome—would destroy the Seleucids and liberate Israel (Dan. 7:13). It could happen after "seventy weeks," that is, 490 years from the Babylonian exile, or about 107 BC, in a clever use of Jeremiah's seventy years. The son of man in Daniel 8:17 is the author. Antioch IV was Gog (Dan. 11:36). The last chapter expresses hopes for the end of the world and resurrection (Dan. 12). A later writer added to the Septuagint version some verses in chapter 3, and two more chapters.

The book of Daniel fueled the hope of supernatural intervention. The apocryphal books of 1 and 2 Enoch were written about this time. In 1 Enoch, the son of man is a god. Wicked angels rebelled. The son of man would come down from heaven with legions of angels who would destroy earthly armies and wicked empires. The messiah lived before the world and will judge all mortals in its last day. In 2 Enoch, Enoch ascended to heaven to meet God. He saw the wheels which made the sun and moon revolve around the earth. Enoch saw angels incessantly singing praises of God, and prisoners awaiting judgement. Satanail was an angel who sought to become God's equal, but was thrown down with his angels. Time will end when the present age ends.

The Maccabean Revolt and the Hasmonean Dynasty

The Hasidim led the people to disobey the orders of Antiochus IV. Many were put to death. The priest Mattathias, son of Hasmon, and his five sons refused to sacrifice to Zeus. Their rebellion sparked the Maccabean war, named after Mattathias' son Judas, called Maccabeus (Hammer). Judas became leader when his father died. He took Jerusalem and rededicated the temple to Yahweh, the first Hanukkah, in 164 BC. The war went on for years. Jonathan succeeded Judas as leader and became high priest by decree in 152 BC.

The apocryphal 2 Maccabees was written in Alexandria about this time. It explained why the faithful were persecuted (God has his plans) and promised that they would be resurrected. Martyrs would receive great rewards in heaven.

After Jonathan's death, Onias III's family was declared extinct to enable Simon, the last surviving son of Mattathias, to replace him. Simon was acclaimed commander and high priest of Judah in a great assembly of the people in 140 BC. The apocryphal 1 Maccabees was completed about 134 BC. It was parallel to 2 Maccabees but was more comprehensive. These books reflected the views of the Hasidim, the backbone of the revolution.

Simon's son, John Hyrcanus, conquered most of Palestine. He occupied Idumea (Edom) and forced the people to convert to Judaism. He took lands in the Transjordan and destroyed the Samaritan temple on Mount Gerizim in 129 BC.

Alexander Jannaeus, Hyrcanus' son, expanded Israel's borders to nearly those of Solomon's kingdom. He was a savage ruler. He crucified eight hundred Jews in Jerusalem and slaughtered their wives and children before their eyes. Thousands fled Judah. The Essenes, objecting to forms of worship, split off from the Hasidim at this time. The Essenes are believed to have occupied the extensive community near the Dead Sea where many scrolls were found, as well as Kochba near Damascus and other settlements. Alexander Jannaeus was probably the "teacher of wickedness" mentioned in the Dead Sea scrolls. The remaining Hasidim became the Pharisees and wielded great influence in the temple. The Hasmonean family continued to rule as high priests until the Jewish war.

Agitation Against the Roman Empire

Pompey captured Jerusalem for Rome in 63 BC. A period of turmoil followed as patriots tried to throw off the Romans, and robbers exploited the disorder. Hezekiah led a band along the Syrian border until the Arab, Herod the Great, killed them. He crushed the resistance, so the Romans made him king. He ruled through brutality.

In Herod's last sickness in 4 BC, two Pharisee rabbis, Judas bar Sepphoraeus and Matthias bar Margalus, suggested removing the golden eagle, symbol of Rome's dominion, from over the great gate to the temple. The rabbis promised eternal bliss in heaven for any who died in the attempt. A group of students lowered themselves with ropes to hack the eagle down. Forty were arrested and brought to Herod. He burned alive the rabbis and those who had climbed down the ropes, and executed the rest.

The Assumption of Moses was written soon after Herod's death. This apocryphal book represented the last words of Moses to Joshua. It was written to help the Jews keep faith as the world approached its end.

Herod willed his kingdom to his three sons, Archelaus, Antipas, and Philip. Archelaus inherited Judea, Samaria, and Idumea. He tried to rule kindly, but the people wanted a Jewish king. When a riot broke out in Jerusalem at passover, Archelaus sent an army into the crowds, killing many, and thus broke up the feast.

Herod's sons went to Rome for confirmation. In Jerusalem, fighting broke out between Roman soldiers and angry pilgrims to the pentecost ceremonies. The great colonnades of the temple were burned. Many died. Two thousand rebels, formerly Herod's soldiers, assaulted Herod's army. Other patriots and outlaws rose up throughout the nation, either to liberate Israel or to exploit the disorder. Many claimed to have power from God. Simon, one of Herod's slaves, crowned himself and led a large pack to rob and burn the palace in Jericho and many other fine homes. Athrongaeus, a shepherd, put on a crown and made his four brothers generals of a roving army that attacked Romans and anyone who might have money. Herod's troops and Roman soldiers destroyed those bands. Galilee was a hotbed of revolt. Judas son of Hezekiah the outlaw raided Herod's armory in Sepphoris and armed a large gang in hope of taking Herod's throne for a free Israel. Varus, Roman legate of Syria, brought an army to destroy Sepphoris and enslave the residents. He razed other villages in Galilee, crucified two thousand men, and pacified the country.

There was an island of peace, reason, and kindness in Galilee. Hillel, in his academy in Tiberias, taught that God was love and reason. Life was sacred, for it came from God. Therefore, human beings were sacred. He taught respect for others: "Do not do to others what you would not have them do to you." Later on he led the Pharisees in Jerusalem. His school brought reason and gentleness into mainstream Judaism.

Herod Antipas inherited Galilee and Peraea (Transjordan). Herod Philip received Iturea in the far north, below Mount Hermon. They ruled well enough, but Rome deposed Archelaus and imposed a governorship over Judea, Samaria, and Idumea. The governors collected taxes for Rome, enriching themselves while impoverishing or dispossessing thousands. Judas of Galilee, a rabbi, founded the patriotic Zealot movement. He argued that paying taxes was serving Rome. Rome was Satan. The Zealot movement grew for decades. "Go catch a fish and give Caesar the gold coin that is in its mouth for both of us" (Mt. 17:27) was a defiant refusal to pay taxes. "Give Caesar what is Caesar's, and God what is God's" (Mark 12:13-17) meant, "Don't pay taxes to Rome—everything is God's," to the Zealots.

Pontius Pilate governed from 26 to 36 AD. He was one of the worst for greed and cruelty. In 27 his army paraded in Jerusalem, displaying the customary emblems: military standards, insignias, and images. Many of the emblems symbolized gods as well as Roman authority, and so the Jews rioted. Pilate hastily withdrew the emblems, but another time he sent men with cudgels into the crowds to suppress rioting. His reign of terror bottled up the mounting anger.

John the baptizer, following in the footsteps of Judas the Galilean and the rabbis who were burned alive, told the people to get ready for the inevitable war against the Romans, for the axe was already set against the roots. He angered the high priests, saying that the Jews did not have to go to the temple to sacrifice; they only had to repent and obey God, and he performed a cleansing ritual in the Jordan. The desperately poor, the dispossessed, the patriots thronged to him. He probably intended to reestablish a free nation, a New Israel. John's interfering with temple collections angered the high priests, and his large crowds worried all authorities. Herod Antipas caught and executed him. John's followers gave him a martyr's burial. Many believed that he had supernatural powers and that he would return to rule Israel as messiah. The cult of John the baptizer probably fled Palestine in the Jewish war. Apparently it persists in Iraq and Iran today as the Mandaeans.

Some of John's followers were determined to carry on his revolt. Jesus of Nazareth summoned Simon Barjona

("Terrorist"), better known as Peter; John and James, Sons of Thunder or Rage; Simon the Zealot (Luke 6:15; Mark 3:17; Mt. 16:17). The rebellion would be bloody (see Mt. 10:34). Crucifixion was the common Roman penalty for revolt (Pick up your cross and follow me!).

Jesus' followers thought he had power from God (Acts 5:34-39) that assured a successful revolt. Jesus said, "I cast out devils and I do cures" (Luke 13:32); he made a living by exorcising demons from people with mental illnesses. So did the disciples: "Even the devils are subject to us through your name" (Luke 10:17). His friends claimed that Baalzebul, a traditional god of healing, lived in him and in them (Mark 3:23-27; 2 Kings 1:2). Their clients believed it (Mark 1:23-27), and his signs of madness proved it (Mark 3:21, 30). Possession of the servant spirit led Jesus and his friends to think that they were above the Jewish law. Educated people charged that Jesus "casts out devils by the prince of devils" (Mt. 9:34). Jesus' friends believed that his spirit had come from heaven and would ensure success in overthrowing the high priests and the Romans. They anointed Jesus (John 12:3) and acclaimed him king (Mark 11:9-10). But the peaceful triumphal march into Jerusalem did not deliver the kingdom to them. A day or so later, Jesus and his followers assaulted the temple (Mark 11:15-19). The insurrection was bloody, and some of the rebels were caught (Mark 15:7). Jesus was later caught in a surprise attack by a superior force despite his friends' swords (Luke 28:36, 38; Mark 14:47). Jesus was accused, convicted, and executed with two others for leading a revolt to overthrow Roman rule. His body disappeared over the sabbath and passover day, and some claimed that they saw him walking around, which confirmed and amplified their belief in his supernatural powers. They expected him to complete the revolt with armies of angels from heaven, to rule the New Israel. He would return very soon; there wasn't even time to notify all the towns of Israel (Mt. 27:64; Luke 19:11). It is likely that Pilate ordered Jesus' body buried in a common grave rather than let it inspire another martyr cult like John's. But a new cult developed and spread, especially among the very poor. James, brother of Jesus and a lower priest, quickly became one of the leaders. He brought Pharisees into the movement; many would have sympathized with any peasants revolt, but they also carried Hillel's pacifism and gentleness with them. James and the Pharisees made the Galileans conform outwardly to Pharisaic ritual, and thus helped make the new cult sufficiently respectable.

The high priest tried to stop the movement, fearing that it would become violent and give Pilate an excuse to slaughter the crowds. He hired Saul of Tarsus to intimidate the congregations of freedmen (former slaves) and hellenistic Jews. But the refugees spread the cult to Jewish populations in Alexandria, Damascus, Antioch, and elsewhere. Sent to Damascus to bring refugees to trial, Saul had what he called a revelation from Jesus. Some think he had an epileptic fit or heatstroke. Saul became a believer; indeed, he elevated Jesus to God the creator, ruler, and destroyer of the universe. The disciples rejected Saul and his new doctrine, but Saul claimed that his revelation made him a better apostle than the disciples.

Caligula proclaimed himself a god, the Younger Gaius, Jupiter the Glorious, and had statues of himself installed everywhere for people to worship throughout the empire. But the Jews fought the installation in Palestine. In the winter of 39-40 AD, Caligula sent an army to install it in the temple in Jerusalem even if it meant wholesale slaughter. The people thought that Caligula was Gog bringing on the end of the world; the "Little Apocalypse" (Mark 13) was written while the army stalled for time. When Caligula was murdered, the army returned to Syria. Nevertheless, "this generation will not pass away before these things are done" (Mark 13:30). Caligula, reigning forty-six months, may be the first beast (Rev. 13:1-9).

In 44 AD, Theudas gathered a crowd to march into Jerusalem, but the Romans killed him and slaughtered his mob. Evidently the Christian Zealots rose up, for Herod Agrippa executed James, Son of Rage, and imprisoned Peter for execution after passover (Acts 5:34; 12:1-19). A friend let Peter escape, and Peter denounced "Pharisees and Herodians." Probably the Pharisees had attacked Peter for fomenting rebellion and for teaching that the law was passè (Mark 8:15). James the brother of Jesus became head of the church. He was a peacemaker. "Turn the other cheek, love your enemies, bless those who curse you" may be James' words, and Hillel's. The letter of James expresses Jewish Christian views, not Paul's: obey the whole law, or else faith is worthless. The poor will be uplifted, the rich cast down. Anger achieves nothing. Don't curse others. The Judge waits at the gates; he will enter at any moment. The Jerusalem church may have been the Jewish Christian sect called the Ebionites (the poor; Gal. 2:10). The Ebionites regarded Jesus as an ordinary man, the son of a man and woman.

Saul was invited to Antioch to evangelize about 46 AD; he went on to Cyprus, Asia Minor, Macedonia, Greece, Rome. He became popular with the hellenists and Gentiles. He disregarded the Jewish law, holding that Jesus' victory over the gods had made it obsolete. He baptized Gentiles directly without circumcision or instruction in Judaism. Thus Paul angered orthodox Jews and Jewish Christians. Christianity was, after all, a Jewish sect; if Gentiles wanted to become Christians, they had to become Jews first. Paul fought with the disciples, accusing Peter of hypocrisy. He wrote much of this in his letter to the Galatians about 48 AD.

Paul's readiness to abandon the Jewish law suggests that he was a Gentile converted to Judaism, despite claims of Jewish birth. As a boy in Tarsus he could have studied philosophies such as Stoicism and the resurrection cult of Attis. Stoicism taught that the world is not permanent, so ignore it; it will pass, but the soul will live on. His ideas about Jesus' crucifixion were probably influenced by the myth of Attis, the god who was sacrificed and resurrected as a fir tree in spring equinoctial festivities. Paul probably spent three years in Kochba, an Essene community in the Arabian Desert near Damascus. If so, he was probably indoctrinated into gnostic cosmology and angelology. Gnosticism permeates his doctrine: the world is evil, ruled by evil angels. Jesus is not just king of Israel, but saviour of the world; he deceived the ruling gods into crucifying him. Jesus would shortly take the souls of the faithful to God's domain and destroy the universe (1 Thess. 4:13-18; 1 Cor. 15:20-28; Gal. 4:3; 1 Cor 2:8). Paul's gospel was foreign to Jesus' disciples, main-line Judaism, and the Jerusalem church. Without Paul, there would be no Christianity today; it would have died out with the Jewish Christian sects. Christianity is a Gentile religion. Paul created it.

Paul's letters and Acts give us a most precious view of his conflicts with the Jewish Christians, though it is all told from his side. Writing from Corinth, Paul assured the Thessalonians that the emperor (either the aged Claudius or Nero, crowned in 54) was not Gog (2 Thess. 2:3).

In Ephesus Paul wrote three letters to the Corinthians (reassembled with a fourth incorrectly to give us 1 and 2 Corinthians). His second letter told of his unresolved conflicts with the disciples. Ephesus expelled him for angering the Jews faithful to the law. He wrote the Romans from Corinth.

The Jews' hostility escalated against the renegade. Paul went to Jerusalem to explain his doctrine. Interestingly, a new messiah, a Jew from Egypt, had just tried to capture Jerusalem and was still at large. The Jerusalem church shunned Paul, and the Jews rioted against him for violating the law. The Romans kept him in protective custody for two years. Then he demanded to be judged by Caesar Nero as a Roman citizen, for Rome was noted for its religious tolerance. He arrived in Rome in 62 AD. The Jews of Rome shunned him, so he taught the Gentiles, at his residence, in chains.

That year the high priest executed James, brother of Jesus. Pharisees, Zealots, and Christians (one could be all three) rioted against the high priest, and the nation was headed for rebellion.

In Rome, Paul wrote letters to the Laodiceans (lost), Colossians, Philemon, and 1 Timothy. Toward the end he wrote the Philippians and boasted of converting Nero's soldiers.

The year 64 AD was a bad one for Christians in Rome. In July a fire destroyed a large part of the city. Nero was accused of starting the fire. He blamed the growing Christian population and put many of them to death. Nero got away with the murders, for the Romans generally suspected Christians of sedition as well as black magic. Peter may have dictated 1 Peter at this time: "Your enemy stalks like a roaring lion for someone to devour." The tradition is that Peter and his wife were crucified, and that Paul was beheaded.

Nero was Gog. An unknown Jewish Christian predicted Nero's death, Rome's fall, and the world's end. A messiah would judge the world. That prediction was added to a Jewish treatise probing God's justice and the unfairness of life (2 Esdras 11:13). Around 100 AD, three chapters were added to the Latin version to assure the reader that the end was even closer than ever before.

The book of Revelation, or the Apocalypse of John, was probably written before Nero died in 68 AD. The first beast was probably Caligula; the second, Nero (Rev. 13:5, 11-18). The scorpions (Rev. 9) were Parthians, skilled archers on horseback in central Asia who humiliated the Romans in 53 BC and might do so again.

The Jewish war broke out in 66 AD. The Zealots made good a promise to destroy bonds of indebtedness and destroy the high priests. Several men backed by rival factions tried to become king; three were to rule Jerusalem through the siege. Probably much of the Jerusalem church had already fled; early writers said that the apostles John, Andrew, and Philip went to Ephesus. Any who stayed to welcome Jesus to Jerusalem died alongside the other patriots. Several Roman legions utterly destroyed Jerusalem in 70 AD. The victors held a great triumphal march in Rome, parading a model of the destroyed temple, pictures and reenactments of the war, enslaved Jewish children, the Torah, and the seven-branched gold lampstand through the streets of Rome.

CHRISTIANITY BECOMES A GENTILE RELIGION

The Jerusalem church was destroyed in the Jewish war, but from the start of the war its control over the churches was ended, and the Gentile churches made their own rules. Gentiles could enjoy hope for eternal life and the mystique of the Jewish tradition of the messiah without the rigor of Jewish rites and instruction. Churches that Paul had established grew rapidly, and new ones appeared everywhere. Gentiles incorporated their idolatry and myths into Christianity. No Jewish sect would have developed a cult of the virgin Mary, nor the dogma of the trinity.

The time for Jesus to appear with his heavenly hosts, if ever he was going to, was when the Romans breached the city walls. But, unimpeded, they destroyed the city and the temple. Most Jewish Christians went back to Judaism. Jewish Christian churches took in Gentiles or withered away.

The Gospels

All four gospels probably contain some material written in the 30's and 40's. The earliest writings were about Jesus the exorcist and rebel, Baalzebul the god who lived in him, and the passing of the Jewish law. They were added to and edited many times. The final versions were written decades later.

Mark. Early authors said that John Mark, nephew of Barnabas and Peter's interpreter in Rome, wrote it down from Peter's sermons. That is plausible, for it was originally written in Aramaic. Mark tried to convince the Jews that Jesus was the son of man who would soon return from heaven with hosts of angels—in their lifetimes—to destroy the Roman armies and rule Israel as a model for the world in an age of peace. This son of man was divine, not a man as in Daniel 7.

The original gospel of Mark was probably much longer. It was kept secret, for it showed that Christians prayed for the return of a rebel (executed by a Roman governor for fomenting revolution) to destroy the Roman empire and liberate Israel.

An editor in the Roman church cut out much material and revised it in 71 AD, after the temple had been destroyed (Mark 13:2). The editor smeared the Jews. He cut all reference to Roman soldiers' capturing Jesus. The gospel of John, in contrast, still has terminology showing that Roman soldiers helped catch him (John 18:3, 12). The editor made the assault on the temple into a lecture. He invented the tale about Peter returning after the disciples fled and wove it into the story. Removing the tale restores the original story. He dissociated Jesus from fellow Zealots who were also captured, especially Barabbas. The editor invented the fable about the ruthless Pilate's releasing Barabbas and trying to please the crowd. His attempts to exonerate the Romans are belied by the inscription on the cross, "King of the Jews," and the Roman soldiers' mocking Jesus for trying to be king. Thus in many ways he made Mark less offensive to the Romans.

This final version of Mark was very popular. Unknown authors expanded it into the gospels of Matthew and Luke about 85 AD. Both gospels also drew on the Q document, which may be the *Sayings of Jesus* attributed to a disciple named Matthew. Examples of Q material are the Lord's prayer (Lk. 11:2-4, Mt. 6:9-13), the beatitudes (Lk. 6:20-23, Mt. 5:3-12); and the parable of the centurion (Lk. 7:1-10, Mt. 8:5-13). **Luke-Acts.** These books were probably written in Greece or Macedonia. Representing Luke as the author and Paul's companion was a fiction suggested by Paul's letters. The author was keenly aware of Domitian's persecutions of Christians and wanted to prove to the Roman rulers that Jesus had truly risen and would return to destroy the world. He used an old gospel probably composed about 50 AD in Caesarea, which began with the present chapter three. He added much material from Mark and Q. Luke transformed the young man in the tomb (Mark 16:5) to two men in shining garments. Acts contains early Jewish Christian documents from Jerusalem, Caesarea, and Antioch. The gospel was separated from Acts when the New Testament was put together.

Matthew. This was written for a large Jewish Christian community, perhaps in Alexandria, as a manual of instruction. It has some unique material that perhaps came from the Jerusalem church. Matthew added the virgin birth based on a mistranslation of "a young woman" in the Septuagint. His three wise men were patterned after Tiridates the king of Armenia and his fellow magicians, who visited Nero. Matthew transformed the young man in Jesus' tomb (Mark 16:5) into an angel and added the earthquake (Mt. 28:2).

John. Early writers said that John the son of Zebedee wrote the gospel, that he settled in Ephesus, and that he was the last of the twelve to die. All of this is possible, though his disciples made additions around 95 AD. Paul's gnostic doctrine influenced the opening hymn (Jesus is eternal, lord, creator, light, God). But John rejects Paul's gnostic belief that the world is evil and God hates it (John 1:1-18; 3:16). The gospel tells much about the servant spirit that entered Jesus and the disciples. The original ending was John 20:30-31.

The last chapter was added to contradict the Jewish Christians who said that he did not rise. It contradicted Paul's gnostic opinion that only Jesus' spirit, not his body, rose. It insisted that John, not Peter, was the chief apostle, for John would not die before Jesus came. John's church, not Rome, should be the mother church. John's church was likely a remnant of the Jerusalem church, settled in Ephesus long after Paul died.

Revelation. Emperor Domitian was another Gog, and the book of Revelation was completed in response to his persecutions in western Asia Minor about 95 AD. Much of the imagery is from Daniel. Babylon represented Rome; Megiddo represented the destruction of great empires (Rev. 16:12-21; Zech. 12:11). Gog and Magog would be thrown into a lake of burning sulfur (Rev. 20:1-10). A new Jerusalem would descend to earth from heaven, and Jesus would come very soon.

The Jewish Christian letter of Jude is dated at about 100 AD. The writer knew 1 Enoch (Jude 6-14), The Testaments of the Twelve Patriarchs (Jude 7), and The Assumption of Moses (Jude 9).

THE CANONS

An Expanded Jewish Canon. After the Romans destroyed Jerusalem, Pharisee scholars established an academy at Jamnia, a town west of Jerusalem. The academy became the Jewish center of learning and government. The scholars kept out Christians and other heretics.

The Jewish literature had become so vast and diverse that one could prove anything by choosing his books. It was hard to keep young minds from false books like Maccabees that advocated the violence that had led to the destruction of Jerusalem. The scholars wanted to teach more than the Torah, and there were many sacred books, such as the prophets and the psalms of David, in danger of becoming lost in the mass of literature. So they enlarged the canon. They agreed that Ezra and Nehemiah were the last prophets. Therefore, God had not spoken through the Hasmoneans, John the baptizer, or Jesus of Nazareth.

For inclusion in the canon, all books had to have been written no later than Ezra and Nehemiah, and they had to be in Hebrew. These criteria kept out the Talmud and the Mishnah, commentaries on the sacred books. Also some inspiring books such as the Martyrdom of Isaiah, 1 Enoch (he "walked with God" and revealed many mysteries), and Jubilees (a retelling of some Genesis and Exodus stories and revelations of Moses to show the truth and universality of his laws). And the many writings about John the baptizer and Jesus of Nazareth were excluded.

The expanded Jewish canon included three classes of scripture. The Torah or Five Books of Moses remained the most hallowed of the sacred books. The Prophets included the Former Prophets (Joshua, Judges, and Kings including Samuel) and the Latter Prophets (Isaiah, Jeremiah, Ezekiel, and the Book of the Twelve). The Book of the Twelve included Hosea, Joel, Amos, Obadiah, Jonah, Micah, Nahum, Habakkuk, Zephaniah, Haggai, Zechariah, and Malachi. The Writings were the least sacred of the canon. They included Psalms, Proverbs, Job, the Five Scrolls (Song of Songs, Ruth, Lamentations, Ecclesiastes, and Esther), Daniel, Ezra, Nehemiah, and Chronicles. Daniel is the only apocalypse in the Jewish canon. The scholars included it because its allegorical style led them to think that it had been written in the exile or the Persian period.

The Jewish canon has not changed since about 100 AD: Torah, Prophets, and Writings. Christians accept it as the Old Testament.

The Apocalyptic Canons

The Christian Bible. The New Testament is the most detailed collection of apocalyptic books. The books were written by 100 AD along with many others and more being written. Each church selected its sacred scriptures in accordance with its particular divine guidance, and they fought each other without mercy. Strong churches searched others for heretical books and burned them. Slaughter was not uncommon. Churches tended to become more gnostic as time went on, with many variations; some believed that souls could escape the wicked world only through asceticism, others by performing every kind of evil. The New Testament canon seems to have been agreed on when Eusebius discussed in 305-325 the profusion of gospels and epistles.

Emperor Constantine proclaimed Christianity the state religion to unify the Roman empire. But churches were fighting each other about gospels and different notions of God, Jesus, and the second coming. Each church was ruled by its own bishop and presbyters. Constantine called the bishops to Nicea in 325 AD to adopt a single creed. Arius led a small majority who held that God is one, unknowable, and creator of all living things. He created Jesus to redeem humanity, so Jesus was not self-existent, eternal, nor truly divine. Athanasius led a group deeming that Jesus was of the same substance as God, coeternal, inseparable, and both fully divine and fully human. Fighting became more bitter for two years, until Constantine ordered the bishops to agree that Jesus was fully divine. He pointed out that Roman emperors were the incarnation of the sun god, the highest god. Since the emperor is divine, Jesus must also be divine. He kept up pressure until the bishops gave in to his wishes. He had statues made of Jesus, resembling himself, for people to worship. So everyone worshipped Constantine as God and as Jesus, and they were united behind him and the empire.

Emperor Theodosius called a conference in 381 AD in which the holy spirit was distinguished as a part of a trinity: father, son, and holy ghost. The church became trinitarian.

Church and empire were thus married, and they strengthened each other. But earthly matters had seriously blemished the religion. The Arian view that God is one was branded as a heresy and persecuted throughout the Roman empire. Arianism persisted among Germanic tribes as unitarianism.

The canon was closed by Jerome's time. Jerome revised the existing Latin translations 382-405 AD. The Old Testament had been taken from the Septuagint, so it included books outside the Jewish canon such as 2 Esdras and 1, 2 Maccabees, which promised eternal life for the faithful. He found the Septuagint unsatisfactory and turned to the Hebrew text. He created a *Hexapla* that presented four different Greek texts and the Hebrew text in both Hebrew and Greek. His use of the Hebrew text angered many in the church. But Jerome's translation, the Vulgate, became the standard and was decreed the exclusive authority at the Council of Trent in 1546. His New Testament included the same books as in Bibles of Roman, Orthodox, and Protestant sects today. But the Eastern Syrian church canon does not include Revelation or letters of James, Peter, and Jude. The Ethiopian church canon includes 2 Esdras, Jubilees, Ascension of Isaiah, and several other apocryphal books.

The Koran. At Mecca the Quraysh tribe worshipped Allah (Elohim), the chief of the gods of their ancestors, at a square stone building which their ancestor Abraham had built. Judaism and Christianity were also established here, deep in Arabia. Mohammed, a well-travelled merchant of the Quraysh tribe, apparently was influenced by local skeptics who disliked the endless discussions of the Jews and despised the polytheism and idolatry of the Christians and Arabs. They advocated return to the asceticism and monotheism of Noah, Abraham, and Moses as represented in the Torah.

Mohammed often meditated and prayed in a nearby cave. About 610 AD the angel Gabriel began to reveal God's wishes to him. Mohammed wrote his revelations on any available material such as stones and leaves, until his death in 632. His revelations were collected and canonized as the Koran within twenty years. The Koran is the source of inspiration for Islam, which means "absolute submission to God's will." Islam regards Mohammed as the last prophet. Jesus was also a prophet, a man, not God or son of God. God is one. He will destroy the world, send the wicked to hell, reward the righteous in heaven. The Koran extended compassion and justice to women and orphans.

Translation of the Bible into European languages. Many wanted to bring the Bible to the people in their own languages. A Gothic translation was done for the Germans about 400 AD. Wycliffe produced the earliest English translation in 1382. Without printing presses or church support, these attempts were short-lived.

Protestant Bibles. Wycliffe omitted from his Old Testament the eleven books rejected by the Jewish canon but accepted by the Roman Catholic Church. These are the Apocrypha, "secret," though they never were secret. Martin Luther omitted them from his 1534 translation. The first edition of the King James Version (1611) included the Apocrypha, but later Protestant Bibles often dropped them. Catholic versions are now beginning to leave them out. Many other interesting noncanonical books written by the middle of the second century were regarded as apocryphal or lost, but were omitted simply because they did not advance church doctrine as well as the chosen books.

The Book of Mormon. Joseph Smith, Jr., was known as a treasure-digger who located treasure through a "luminary peepstone." In 1830, he said that he translated the book of Mormon from golden plates which the angel Moroni revealed to him. They were the record of the prophet Mormon of Jesus' teachings to a Hebrew tribe who came to America. The plates vanished, but three of his followers testified to seeing them as well as Moroni. The book of Mormon and the Old and New Testaments are the canon of the Church of Jesus Christ of Latter-day Saints. Smith has been accused of basing his book of Mormon on a novel by another person.

Christian Science. Relieving her own chronic disorders by reading the New Testament, Mary Baker Eddy rediscovered the methods by which Jesus healed. From those principles she wrote *Science and Health* in 1875, organized the Church of Christ, Scientist, in 1879, and founded the Massachusetts Metaphysical College in 1881. The book, revised as *Science and Health with Key to the Scriptures*, is church canon along with the Bible.

Any More Bibles?

We are still in the age of apocalypse, for millions of people all over the world expect the world to end at any time. Also, charismatic figures turn up every so often to tell the world about their revelations and unseen powers. Usually they produce books about their revelations. As time goes on, some of the most popular books of this type will be canonized. They will become the Bibles of the new faiths. The age of writing Bibles is not over.

Further Reading

Most of us read the Bible in hope of understanding what the authors intended to say. Priests and scholars often disagree, so ultimately each of us has to make up his or her own mind. The present volume is the barest introduction, and many of the glib statements given here are controversial. The search for meaning takes us into archaeology, ancient history, myths, literature, languages, philosophy, the beginnings of science. And so on. No one person can be expert in all the subjects, but any of us can have a passing familiarity of the most important fields appropriate to our personal search. And the search is immensely interesting. The following references are only a few of the many that can illuminate our search.

AARON, Kevin James, 1989. Journey from Eden. Cathedral Publications, iv + 212 pp.

APULEIUS. With tr. by W. Adlington, 1566; rev., G. Gaselee, 1915. The golden ass, being the metamorphoses of Lucius Apuleius. Harvard University Press, 608 pp. Illustrate some ancient religious notions and practices, notably with a troop peddling favors of the Syrian goddess and Lucius' induction into the Isis cult (Bk. 8,11).

ASIMOV, Isaac, 1971. Asimov's guide to the Bible. Vol. I, The Old Testament. Vol. II, The New Testament. Avon Publishers. Gives the history and meaning of each book, including Apocrypha.

BARTHEL, Manfred, 1980. Tr., Wm. Morrow Co., 1982. What the Bible really says: casting new light on the book of books. Quill, Wm. Morrow Co., 413 pp.

BIGGER, Stephen, ed., 1989. Creating the Old Testament; emergence of the Hebrew Bible. Basil Blackwell, xx + 364 pp.

BRANDON, S.G.F., 1967. Jesus and the Zealots. Scribner, 1975 ed. Presents evidence that Jesus tried to overthrow the government and was executed for rebellion.

BRANDON, S.G.F., 1968. The trial of Jesus of Nazareth. Scarborough: Stein and Day, N.Y., 1979 ed., 223 pp. A condensation of *Jesus and the Zealots*.

BULFINCH, Thomas, 1855. The age of fable. New American Library, 1962 ed., 408 pp.

BULTMANN, Rudolf, and Karl Kundsin, 1934. Tr., F.C. Grant. Form criticism: two essays on New Testament research. Reprint 1962, Harper Torchbooks, 161 pp.

CAIRD, G.B., 1963. The gospel of St. Luke. Penguin, 267 pp.

CORNFELD, Gaalyah, ed., 1961. Adam to Daniel: an illustrated guide to the Old Testament and its background. Macmillan, 559 pp.

EUSEBIUS. Tr., G.A. Williamson, 1965. The history of the church from Christ to Constantine. Penguin, 429 pp.

FAST, Howard, 1968. The Jews: story of a people. Dell, reprint 1982. 380 pp.

FISHBANE, Michael, 1985. Biblical interpretation in ancient Israel. Reprint 1989, Clarendon Press, Oxford University, xviii + 617 pp.

FORBES, Milton L., 1989. The Messiah. Mountaintop Books, xvi + 272 pp.

FRAZER, James George, 1963. The golden bough; a study in magic and religion. Macmillan.

FRIEDMAN, Richard Elliott, 1987. Who wrote the Bible? Summit Books. 299 pp. Argues identity of Dtr[1], Dtr[2], and R, and existence of JE and P torahs. *Presents sources of entire Torah.* Describes the tabernacle in Solomon's temple, provides many other insights. Essential for the student.

GABEL, J.B., and C.B. Wheeler, 1989. The Bible as literature, Oxford U. Press, 304 pp. Presents literary forms, history, conditions, translations.

GILL, Dan, 1991. Subterranean waterworks of Biblical Jerusalem: adaptation of a karst system. Science, 254:1467-1471.

GINZBERG, Louis, 1956. The legends of the Bible. Simon and Schuster, 646 pp.

GOODSPEED, Edgar J., 1938. The Apocrypha. Reprint, Vintage Books, 1959, xxvi + 493 pp.

GUTHRIE, W.C.K., 1951. The Greeks and their gods. Beacon Press, 388 pp.

HADAS, Moses, and Morton Smith, 1965. Heroes and gods. Routledge and Kegan Paul, Ltd., London, 266 pp.

HEIDEL, Alexander, 1942. The Babylonian Genesis. University of Chicago Press, Phoenix ed., 1963, x + 153 pp. + 12 pls.

HELMS, Randel, 1988. Gospel fictions. Prometheus Books, 154 pp.

HOMER. The Iliad.

JONAS, Hans, 1963. The gnostic religion, ed. 2 rev. Reprint 1970, Beacon Press, Boston, xx + 358 pp.

JOSEPHUS. Tr., G.A. Williamson, 1959. The Jewish war. Penguin, 425 pp.

KORAN. Tr., N.J. Dawood, 1956. Penguin, vii + 456 pp.

KRAMER, Samuel Noah, 1963. The Sumerians. University of Chicago Press, 355 pp.

KRUPP, Edwin C., 1983. Echoes of the ancient skies: the astronomy of lost civilizations. Harper and Row, 386 pp. Ancient configurations of celestial bodies are recorded in some myths.

LAROUSSE, 1968. New Larousse encyclopedia of mythology. Hamlyn Publishing Group, Ltd., 500 pp.

LOST BOOKS OF THE BIBLE, 1926. First published as *The Apocryphal New Testament*. Tr., Jeremiah Jones and William Wake, 1820. Reprint 1979, Bell Publishing Co., 293 pp. Includes Mary, Infancy of Jesus, Lost gospel according to Peter.

MACCOBY, Hyam, 1987. The mythmaker: Paul and the invention of Christianity. Harper and Row, xii + 237 pp. He shows Paul's Gentile connections and how he invented Christianity.

MAGNUSSON, Magnus, 1977. Archaeology of the Bible. Simon and Schuster, 239 pp. Tells about the Ebla tablets and much else.

MANSON, T.W., 1948. The teaching of Jesus. Cambridge University Press.

MANSON, T.W., 1949. The sayings of Jesus. SCM Press, London, 347 pp.

MEYER, Marvin W., tr., 1984. The secret teachings of Jesus: four gnostic gospels. Vintage, Random House, xxii +131 pp.

NEILL, Stephen, 1976. Jesus through many eyes. Fortress Press, 214 pp.

NEW JERUSALEM BIBLE, 1985. Doubleday, xvi + 2120 pp. + 7 pls., cloth. Makes full use of scholarship, Greek and Hebrew texts, has copious footnotes and extensive introductions to all books. Renders YHWH as Yahweh. Based on work of Bible Studies Institute, Jerusalem. Paperback edition lacks footnotes and introductions.

PEARLMAN, Moshe, 1973. The Maccabees. Macmillan, 272 pp.

PLATT, Rutherford H., Jr., 1980. The forgotten books of Eden. Bell, reprint of 1927 ed. xii + 269 pp. Includes apocryphal books such as 1, 2 Book of Adam and Eve, Secrets of Enoch, Odes of Solomon, Testaments of the Twelve Patriarchs.

POTOK, Chaim, 1978. Wanderings: history of the Jews. Fawcett, 576 pp.

REALE, Giovanni, 1985. A history of ancient philosophy, v. 3. The systems of the hellenistic age. Tr., John R. Catan. State University of New York Press, 499 pp.

ROBINSON, John Mansley, 1968. An introduction to early Greek philosophy. Houghton Mifflin, Boston, 342 pp.

SCHOLEM, Gershom, 1974. Kabbalah. New American Library, 494 pp.

SCHWEITZER, Albert, 1906. The quest of the historical Jesus. Reprint, 1948, Harper and Row.

SMITH, Morton, 1973. The secret gospel. Harper and Row, 148 pp. Presents evidence of a lost, older, long version of Mark.

SMITH, Morton, 1978. Jesus the magician. Harper and Row, 222 pp. Shows the meaning of Jesus' exorcisms and explains why he became known as a magician and god.

SOGGIN, J. Alberto, 1985. A history of ancient Israel. Westminster/Knox, xviii + 436 pp.

SOGGIN, J. Alberto, 1989. Introduction to the Old Testament. Ed. 3. Westminster/Knox, 608 pp.

SPONG, John Shelby, 1991. Rescuing the Bible from fundamentalism: a bishop rethinks the meaning of scripture. HarperCollins Publishers, xvi + 267 pp.

TYSON, Joseph B., 1973. A study of early Christianity. Macmillan, 446 pp.

VERMES, G., 1968. The Dead Sea scrolls in English. Penguin, ed. 2, 281 pp.

WRIGHT, George Ernest, 1962. Biblical archaeology. Westminster, Philadelphia, 291 pp.

ZIMMERMANN, Frank, 1979. The Aramaic origin of the four gospels. KTAV Publishing House, 244 pp.

Order Blank

Quant.	Title	Author	Price	Extension
	Out of the Mists of Time...paper	Forbes	4.95	
	The Messiah cloth	Forbes	29.95	
	The Messiah paper	Forbes	19.95	
Subtotal				
Iowa residents please add 4% tax				
Shipping, per order				2.00
Total				

Prices subject to change without notice.
Please remit by check or money order, US funds only to:

Mountaintop Books
PO Box 385
Glenwood, IA 51534-0385

Ship to: Date:

_____
Name

_____
Street address or box number

_____
City   State   Zip code